W9-BNO-031

GILDING

Easy Techniques
& Elegant Projects
with Metal Leaf

Jane LaFerla

WITHDRAWN

Jefferson-Madison
Regional Library
Charlottesville, Virginia

Sterling Publishing Co., Inc.
New York

1501 3319

ART DIRECTOR: **Chris Bryant**
PHOTOGRAPHER: **Evan Bracken**
PRODUCTION: **Chris Bryant, Bobby Gold**
Photo page 44 (origami butterflies): Tim Barnwell

Library of Congress Cataloging-in-Publication Data

LaFerla, Jane.
  Gilding : easy techniques & elegant projects with metal leaf / Jane LaFerla
      p.   cm.
  "A Sterling / Lark Book."
  Includes index.
  ISBN 0-8069-9554-8
  1. Gilding. I. Title.
TT380.L34   1997
745.7'5—dc21   96-48695
                                                              CIP

10 9 8 7 6 5 4 3 2 1

A Sterling/Lark Book

Published by Sterling Publishing Co., Inc.
  387 Park Ave. South, New York, NY 10016

Created and produced by Altamont Press, Inc.
  50 College St., Asheville, NC 28801

© 1997, Altamont Press

Distributed in Canada by Sterling Publishing,
  c/o Canadian Manda Group, One Atlantic Ave., Suite 105, Toronto, Ontario, Canada M6K 3E7

Distributed in Great Britain and Europe by Cassell PLC,
  Wellington House, 125 Strand, London, England WC2R 0BB

Distributed in Australia by Capricorn Link (Australia) Pty Ltd.,
  P.O. Box 6651, Baulkham Hills Business Centre, NSW, Australia 2153

The written instructions, photographs, designs, patterns, and projects in this volume are intended for the personal use of the reader and may be reproduced for that purpose only. Any other use, especially commercial use, is forbidden under law without written permission of the copyright holder.

Every effort has been made to ensure that all the information in this book is accurate. However, due to differing conditions, tools, and individual skills, the publisher cannot be responsible for any injuries, losses, or other damages that may result from the use of the information in this book.

Printed in Hong Kong

All rights reserved

ISBN 0-8069-9554-8

CONTENTS

Introduction

Faux Malachite Chest
Instructions on page 54.

*S*ay
the word
G I L D I N G, and what do you envision? A golden cherub floating for all eternity on a Rococo ceiling? Treasures from an Egyptian tomb? Aunt Hildy's favorite picture frame?

For most people, gilding evokes an image of opulence in the extreme—the elegant excesses of Louis XIV, for example. To others, it can be a touch of the divine; altar pieces of the early Italian Renaissance take on a heavenly glow that leaves us pining for riches not of this world.

To some, gilding carries a negative connotation. The technique, after all, is a deceit. By fixing thin sheets of beaten gold over an object, the artisan tricks the viewer into believing that the object is more attractive or valuable than it actually is.

Whatever your perception, the pure essence of gilding remains rooted in the magic of transformation. Gilding is an extravagant alchemy that heightens our senses and makes us look at objects in a totally different way. What at first may appear to be a deceit is actually the conceit of the art; we are delightfully fooled, playfully maneuvered into believing that what we see isn't what we think it to be after all.

A GILDING RENAISSANCE

Today's renewed interest in faux finishes and decorative painting has led people to rediscover the art of gilding. Because the application of leaf lends itself to almost any surface and shape, artists and artisans are incorporating it into their work across all mediums.

The idea that leaf is a temperamental material whose application takes exacting techniques may have been keeping you from trying your hand at gilding. This book is designed to help you set aside those preconceived notions. While leaf is delicate, it's not unmanageable, and new materials are making it easier to apply than ever before.

Leaf comes in a variety of metals, offering options in both color and price. These available choices, combined with painted base coats, tinted sealers, or finishing highlights, can give you endless effects.

With a basic understanding of the technique and a willingness to experiment, you can gild just about anything. Consider a touch of gold around a door frame or molding. Imagine candlelight reflected from a golden plate. Recycled pieces, flea-market finds, or the basket you just can't give away lend themselves perfectly to gilding; they get a new life, and you acquire a resurrected treasure to keep or share as a gift.

Polymer Jewelry
Instructions on page 60.

Gilded Chocolate
Instructions on page 91.

CONTEMPORARY APPROACHES TO GILDING

Contemporary gilding, as presented in this book, allows you to use the latest materials to your advantage for quick results on your very first project. You can begin leafing with products found in an art or craft supply shop, the local hardware store, the paint store, and around the house. You'll also find complete leaf supply companies in most large cities.

The projects in this book represent a variety of surfaces for gilding. You can follow the instructions or use them as points of departure for creating your own projects. While each designer essentially follows the same procedures for gilding, their individual instructions allow them to share with you their favorite methods for preparing surfaces, handling leaf, and finishing techniques.

A simple word of caution if you're just starting out: fight the temptation to gild that prized family heirloom as your learning project. Begin by gilding a simple object, to get a feel for working with leaf.

As you continue to explore working with leaf, you'll discover your own touch and find your own short-cuts. Eventually, you may a want to try your hand at the more traditional techniques or carry your interest further by experimenting with other materials and methods.

HISTORY

Gilding dates back at least 4,000 years. The ancient Egyptians used gold leaf as embellishment for furnishings, ritual utensils, and architectural decoration. It was found in temples, tombs, and in the Pharaoh's household. Carved and gilded wooden goddesses stood guard over King Tutankhamen's canopic chests. They were only some of the gold-leafed treasures that accompanied him on his eternal journey. Examples of gilding can be found in other ancient cultures as well, including Greek, Roman, and Chinese.

15TH-CENTURY ITALIAN RELIQUARY; WATER-GILDED GOLD LEAF ON WOOD.

Courtesy of Village Antiques, Asheville, North Carolina.

18TH-CENTURY MIRROR FRAMÉ; WATER-GILDED GOLD LEAF ON CARVED WOOD.

Courtesy of Village Antiques, Asheville, North Carolina.

During the late Middle Ages in Italy, the use of gold leaf became popular for highlighting religious paintings and carvings. Its use in fine art continued until the late Renaissance, when gilding was used less in paintings and more in the decorative arts and as architectural embellishment.

The Baroque and Rococo periods are synonymous with an exuberant, almost giddy, use of gilding; the style is immediately recognizable. Floors, ceilings, columns, moldings, furniture, decorative accessories, and virtually every nook and cranny glowed with shimmering leaf. The sheer volume of gilding done during those times was truly a tribute to the evolved techniques of the craft. Because many gilded items produced during the Baroque and Rococo periods remain in excellent condition, the study of these pieces continues to inspire those interested in gilding techniques.

Over the past 200 years, gilding as a decorative art has waned, though it has continued to enjoy moments of intermittent popularity. Unfortunately, many people have come to think of gilding as an outdated technique used only for restoration or conservation. Today, that perception is changing as more and more people rediscover the transformative power of the craft.

EVOLUTION

Over the centuries, the traditional techniques and materials for gilding have changed very little. The most dramatic advances are fairly recent, having been made in the later decades of the 20th century. New materials and production methods have made gilding more accessible and have opened the craft to a wider range of applications.

The advent of new chemical compounds make user-friendly acrylic gesso and varnishes, latex paint, and synthetic water-based size readily available. Complete systems that simplify the gilding process are currently on the market. Some closely duplicate the high luster of fine water gilding.

Leaf for gilding is produced by successive beatings of the metal that render a final sheet (leaf) approximately 1/200,000 of an inch (.000127 mm) thick. It was once made by hand. Today, computer-monitored hydraulic presses control the process and produce leaf that replicates the look of hand-hammered metal.

17TH-CENTURY FRENCH decorative RELIEF; WATER-GILDED GOLD LEAF ON CARVED WOOD.
Courtesy of Village Antiques, Asheville, North Carolina.

19TH-CENTURY FRENCH SETTEE; WATER-GILDED GOLD LEAF ON CARVED WOOD.
DETAIL: CHIPS IN THE GOLD LEAF REVEAL THE BOLE, GESSO, AND WOOD UNDERNEATH.
Courtesy of Village Antiques, Asheville, North Carolina.

Gilding: The Basics

GILDING can be described as applying a "skin" of thinly beaten metal onto a surface by means of an adhesive known as *size*. At its most developed, gilding is an art form that showcases the exacting skills of a master craftsman. At its simplest, gilding is a sophisticated cousin of the basic cut-and-paste project. If you have a working knowledge of scissors and glue, you're well on your way to learning how to gild.

The results you achieve from gilding are based on the materials you use and the gilding methods you employ. Every project you attempt will have five variables that will affect the finished product in different ways: the surface of the object you're gilding and how you prepare it; the type of leaf you use; the size you use; and any sealer coat or decorative finish you add after you lay the leaf.

The most basic materials you need are size and leaf. Combine these with an understanding of the two methods of gilding—water gilding and oil gilding—and you're almost ready to begin your first project.

Water Gilding vs. Oil Gilding

While the projects in this book follow the procedures for oil gilding, an understanding of water gilding is essential for a complete perspective and appreciation of the craft.

WATER GILDING

Water gilding is a traditional application for wood. The process allows the leaf to be burnished—polished by rubbing—after it's been laid, giving the surface a high, metallic luster that closely imitates polished gold.

First, a coat of *gesso* (chalk powder that is mixed into a liquid medium) is applied to the surface. This serves to seal the wood, hide minor imperfections, and provide a uniform surface for the leaf. If needed, or desired for the finished look, successive layers of gesso are applied, with sanding after each layer to create a smooth, flawless surface. Layers of gesso can also be applied to create raised areas on the surface that can be carved into decorative motifs.

Because traditional gesso is porous, it absorbs the size, which means there's no sticky surface to hold the leaf in place. To prevent this, a clay mixture, known as the *bole*, is applied over the gesso. Bole serves two purposes. It creates a smooth surface that will accept the *gilder's water,* the size that's used in water gilding to bind the leaf to the surface. And it provides a colored base coat.

When held up to the light, leaf is translucent. Bole, which originally came in shades of red and yellow, imparts a tone to the finished piece. Bole also provides a surface color that can be seen through the small cracks known as *faults* (sometimes referred to as *holidays*) that are possible in the leafing process. In contemporary gilding, bole has come to mean any colored base coat applied to a surface to be gilded.

Once the surface is primed with the bole, it is time to apply the leaf, using gilder's water. Gilder's water can be plain water, or water mixed with egg whites, or variations on a recipe that include wood alcohol, water, and a size made from rabbit skin pellets dissolved in water. Throughout history, gilders have prided themselves on their own recipes, often carefully guarding their secrets.

First, the gilder brushes gilding water on a small section of the bole. Then he takes a sheet of metal leaf from its book, using a *gilder's tip*—a flat brush made of long hairs (squirrel or sable) set between pieces of cardboard. If the leaf needs to be cut, it's placed on a *gilder's cushion,* a padded leather surface, and cut with a *gilder's knife.* Using the gilder's tip, the gilder places the leaf on the surface that's been brushed with gilding water and pats the leaf with cotton batting to fix it and smooth it.

Once the leaf is in place and has had time to set, or "dry," the gilder gently brushes away any excess and begins to burnish the surface. This is done with a *burnishing tool,* a smooth stone set in a wooden handle. You can only burnish leaf that has been water-gilded.

OIL GILDING

Oil gilding is much simpler. Its ease of use makes it a natural choice for contemporary applications. It gets its name from the *oil-based size* (sometimes referred to as *resin size*) that is used in the process.

In oil gilding, the size is applied directly to a prepared surface. Then the size is allowed to dry to a point where it becomes *tacky* (sticky) to the touch. The leaf is laid onto the tacky size, which acts as a glue for fixing the leaf. Remember that this process is different from water gilding, where the leaf is laid directly onto the wet gilder's water.

Oil gilding creates a durable surface for distressing, over-painting, and antiquing. You can use it for exterior applications. Since you cannot burnish oil-gilded leaf, oil-gilded objects have more of a matte look when compared to the super-shiny surfaces of water-gilded objects.

A relatively new formula to the craft of gilding is *synthetic water-based size.* This size works exactly like oil size, in that it is applied to a prepared surface and must become tacky before the leaf is laid. Understandably, this often causes some confusion in terms. Using water-based size is not water gilding. Technically, the use of water-based size is considered oil gilding. It helps to think of oil gilding as a method rather than as a descriptive term based on the chemical composition of the size you use.

Metal Leaf

Today there is a wide variety of metal leaf to meet your needs and fit your price range. You can choose from real gold, silver, aluminum, or copper. Composition gold leaf, which is made of brass (copper and zinc), duplicates the many shades of real gold. It is sometimes called Dutch metal or Schlagmetal. Variegated leaf is composition leaf that has been heat-treated to create colorful patterns on its surface. Most of the projects in this book use composition gold, variegated, copper, silver, or aluminum leaf.

REAL GOLD LEAF

Real gold leaf comes in leaves that are 3⅜ inches (85 mm) square. It is packaged in books of 25 leaves with tissue paper separating the leaves. Pure gold leaf is 24-karat gold. The most durable gold leaf is the purest. Adding silver, copper, and other metals to the gold alters its purity and determines its karats. The proportion of metals alloyed to pure gold creates the range of shades available in gold leaf. As the gold leaf decreases in karats and becomes less pure, the shade becomes lighter. When you are using leaf for food projects, it must be as pure as possible and should contain only silver and gold.

The price of real gold leaf fluctuates with the current gold markets. Gold leaf will not tarnish and does not need a sealer coat unless you want to use a sealer as a protective coating.

COMPOSITION LEAF

Composition leaf comes in leaves that are 5½ inches (142 mm) square. Like real gold, it comes in books of 25 leaves with tissue paper separating the individual leaves. Because it is larger and slightly thicker than real gold leaf, composition gold leaf is easier to handle. It is also substantially less expensive and therefore a logical choice for the beginner as well as the serious gilder.

The percentage of copper to zinc in the brass of composition leaf determines its color. It comes in four shades of gold, ranging from deep red-gold to a bright yellow. Because it contains copper, composition leaf must have a sealer coat to prevent tarnishing.

VARIEGATED LEAF

Variegated leaf comes in shades of red, blue, green, multicolor, and black. Although variegated leaf is made from composition gold leaf, it is slightly more expensive because of the treatment it undergoes to create its patterning. Because variegated leaf contains copper, it must also be sealed to prevent tarnishing.

SILVER LEAF

Silver leaf contains only pure silver. Because of this, it tarnishes easily and will need a sealer coat when the leafing is completed. Once applied, silver leaf can be made to look like gold with an application of tinted varnish. This was a popular substitute for the more expensive gold before composition leaf.

COPPER LEAF

Copper leaf is pure copper and needs a sealer coat after application. Its red hue works as a complement to any warm color palette.

ALUMINUM LEAF

Aluminum has a silver color that allows it to substitute for real silver leaf. It is sometimes referred to as composition silver leaf or artificial silver leaf. It does not need a sealer coat but may naturally darken with age.

You will be easily able to find composition, copper, silver, or aluminum leaf at an art or craft supply shop; some may even carry real gold. Most big cities have gilding-supply companies where you can purchase a variety of leaf as well as complete tools and materials for all types of gilding. These companies also offer comprehensive mail-order services. They are more than happy to answer any questions you might have concerning the use and performance of their products and may even be able to help you with some of the finer points of gilding.

PREPARE THE SURFACE.

APPLY THE BOLE.

Gilding in Seven Simple Steps: A Preview

There are seven basic steps to gilding. The complexity of each step is based on the object you'll be gilding and the desired look of the finished project. An antique wood surface will take more preparation than a glass plate, for instance. No matter what you gild, you should get good results by simply following these steps.

This chart is a simple overview of the gilding process. Detailed instructions for gilding begin on page 16.

APPLY THE SIZE.

LAY THE LEAF.

BRUSH THE EXCESS LEAF FROM THE SURFACE.

DISTRESS, DECORATE, OR OVERPAINT THE LEAF (OPTIONAL).

SEAL THE SURFACE.

Materials and Tools

In the description of each step you'll find an explanation of all materials and tools that are specific to that step. There are some basic materials and tools, however, that you will use frequently throughout the gilding process. You may already have many of these around the house. As you gather these items, think in terms of setting up your *gilder's bench*—the name for a gilder's work area.

BRUSHES

If you've done previous art or craft work, you should have enough brushes on hand to begin your projects. You will need brushes for applying base coats, size, and sealers. At various times brushes are also used for laying the leaf, for tamping leaf into crevices, for applying the skewings (small pieces of leaf) to cover faults, for removing excess leaf, and for gently smoothing leaf after it is applied.

If you need brushes, good, moderate-priced ones will serve you well. Don't try to save by buying bargain brushes. They'll shed, leaving behind hairs that will cause you frustration when applying a base or sealer coat. Synthetic brushes work well with latex-based and oil-based products. For objects that involve faux finishes or for covering larger surfaces, you can use standard paint brushes, sponges, or materials available in a paint or hardware store.

Disposable foam brushes, which come in a variety of widths, are particularly useful when working with oil-based paint and size. Rather than clean them, just throw them away.

A 2-inch (5 cm) *bristle brush* works well for brushing off excess leaf. It is also available in other sizes to suit your project needs.

Stencil brushes are stiffer, thick, round brushes for placing, tamping, and smoothing leaf.

You'll need an assortment of *artist's brushes* in natural-hair and natural bristle. If you must have one good brush, make it sable. These brushes seem to have the right body for working with bronze or mica powders and for "faulting" (filling in small cracks).

A *gilder's tip* is a flat brush made of the long hairs of squirrel or sable. It doesn't have a handle like other paint brushes; rather, the hairs are set between two pieces of cardboard. A gilder's tip is a traditional tool used for transferring the leaf to the sized surface. It is not a necessity for contemporary gilding where it's easier to handle the leaf with the tissue paper that comes with the leaf. You may want to try using a gilder's tip to see if it suits your touch.

Basic paint brushes found in paint and hardware stores will be needed for painting larger surfaces or for laying base coats and varnishing.

GLOVES

You should use disposable latex gloves for everything but laying the leaf. Gloves will keep your hands clean of primer and base coats. Remember, size remains tacky for a time.

While the size may appear to be dry on your bare hands, it may still be tacky. This size will pick up any stray pieces of loose leaf or the small pieces of leaf known as skewings. This can be extremely frustrating when you are trying to lay the leaf and is just as annoying as having gum stick to the bottom of your shoe.

NEWSPAPERS

Old newspapers will save your working surface. They absorb water and spills and can be changed and discarded as you go, always giving you a clean work area.

RAGS

You'll want soft, lint-free rags for your gilding projects. Old T-shirts are ideal.

SANDPAPER

Sandpaper is often referred to by its grade, such as coarse, medium, and fine. It is also referred to by numbers that indicated the amount of grit per square inch on the sanding surface: #200 is considered medium grade, while #400 and #600 are fine grades.

SCISSORS

Any sharp, easy-to-handle scissors will serve.

TACK CLOTH

If you're sanding, you will need a tack cloth—a cloth that has been treated with shellac so it is sticky to the touch. It is used to clean small particles of sand, dirt, and debris from a surface.

TAPE

Low-tack painter's tape is a good all-purpose type to use in your projects. It is not as sticky as masking tape and will not harm finished surfaces.

TURNTABLE

A simple turntable is not a necessity but it is certainly convenient. It will minimize your handling of tacky or newly leafed surfaces when you try to get to the other side of an object.

WHITE GLUE

This versatile household glue works on many different surfaces.

STEP 1: Prepare the Surface

THIS step varies according to the composition and condition of the surface you'll be gilding. It's the most important phase of any project (and often the most tedious), since proper preparation not only makes gilding easier but leads to quality results.

To begin, first assess the object's general condition. Then prepare it as if you were going to paint or finish it, repairing the object if necessary and sealing any porous surfaces.

WOOD

Thoroughly clean old finishes or strip them if they're in bad condition. There are many commercial preparations for removing old finishes from wood surfaces. Follow the manufacturer's instructions carefully, since these preparations are often caustic and can harm your skin and eyes. Look for some of the less toxic preparations available today at hardware or paint stores.

If needed, use wood filler to repair small nicks, holes, or flaws in the wood surface prior to sealing or painting the wood. Wood filler, found in hardware or paint stores, is a moist paste that hardens as it dries. Once the filler is dry, you can use sandpaper to remove any excess filler that may remain on the wood surface.

Sand the wood with sandpaper. Always sand in the direction of the wood grain for best results. A first sanding with medium-grit sandpaper will smooth a raised grain or eliminate any leftover finish. A second sanding, using a fine-grit sandpaper, will give you the smooth surface you want for gilding.

Use a tack cloth to remove any loose dirt, small debris, or grit left on the wood surface. If these particles are not removed, they will get trapped underneath the sealer or paint and will create a rough surface that will show through the leaf.

Now the wood surface is ready to seal. To do this, you can use gesso, shellac, or sanding sealer. Gesso is used to seal porous surfaces. It is made from chalk powder (whiting) that is mixed into a liquid medium to become a thick, opaque, white solution. Acrylic-based gesso is easy to find in art or craft supply shops and is ready to use directly from the bottle. While usually found in white, gesso also comes in a few basic colors. If you need to, you can make your own colored gesso by mixing white gesso with dry paint pigments, which are colors in a powder form.

Shellac is an alcohol-based sealer for raw wood that comes in either a white or clear preparation. You can use clear shellac in Step 7 for sealing the gilded surface, but be aware that it may slightly alter the color of the leaf. Shellac is much better for this step.

You may also use sanding sealer to seal raw wood. It penetrates the wood and helps prevent the grain from rising, making the surface smooth enough to accept further finishing coats. Its name comes from its composition—it is easy to sand without gumming the sandpaper. You can find shellac and sanding sealer at hardware or paint stores.

METAL

If the metal object has been previously painted and the finish is in poor condition, use a steel brush to remove chipping paint and rust. Go over the surface again with a medium-grit sandpaper, paying special attention to the rust spots. Clean the surface with a rag, then a tack cloth.

Apply a rust-inhibiting primer coat to seal the metal and prevent any rust from bleeding through subsequent finishes. The primer comes in two preparations, either in cans for application with a brush or as a spray. You can easily find rust-inhibiting primer coats in hardware and paint stores.

You can gild directly over bare metals such as stainless steel and aluminum. Just make sure the metal is clean and free of oil or dirt. Before applying the size, you may want to wipe the metal with a rag dampened with denatured alcohol to clean the surface.

If you plan to paint a metal surface before gilding it, you may have to coat the bare metal with bonding liquid to ensure that the surface will accept the paint. Bonding liquid is a primer coat that prevents paint from chipping off metal surfaces. Applied like paint in either liquid or spray form, it adheres to smooth metal and creates a rough surface that readily accepts paint. It is available at paint, hardware, and automotive supply stores.

LEATHER, VINYL, AND PLASTICS

These materials generally provide a nonporous, sealed surface and are usually ready to accept the bole or leaf size. If you have any doubts, seal the surface with a clear shellac or gesso.

FABRIC AND PAPER

Fiber objects, which include paper, are porous unless treated. To gild them, you need to provide a sealed surface that will prevent the size from being absorbed into the fibers. Gesso works well; it will stiffen fabric and paper. You may also use a spray sealer, also called spray fixative or lacquer. These sealers are available in art and craft supply shops and are used to protect completed paintings or drawings from smudges or dirt. Most often they are acrylic-based and come in matte, satin, or gloss finishes. Spray sealers, formulated for fiber surfaces, are a lighter preparation than shellac. They are not recommended for sealing wood surfaces.

GLASS AND CERAMICS

The surfaces of glass and glazed ceramics are nonporous and are ready to accept the base coat or leaf size.

When you've finished preparing the surface, let the object dry thoroughly before proceeding to Step Two.

Gallery of Gilding

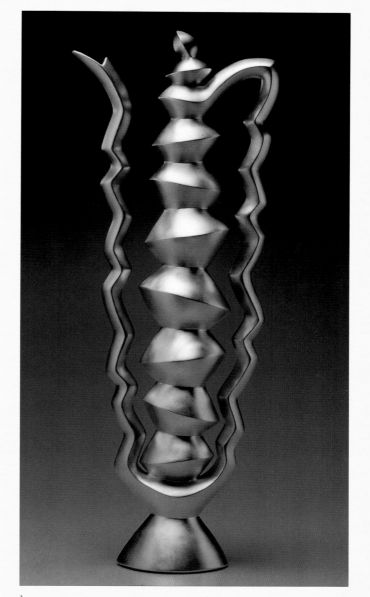

⸖ Jacob's Ladder

MICHAEL SHERRILL AND MARGERY SHERRILL
32" x 14" x 5" (81.5 x 35.5 x 12.5 cm.)
Oil-gilded, 23k gold leaf over a clay body.
PHOTO: **Tim Barnwell**

Step 2: Apply the Bole

ONCE the surface is prepared and dry, you can begin applying the bole—the colored base coat. The bole imparts tone to the leaf and provides a color that will show through any cracks, commonly known as faults or holidays, that may occur when you lay the leaf.

For painting larger surfaces and objects, your local paint store will be able to supply you with alkyd (oil-based) or latex paints in a wide range of colors. If your chosen project involves faux painting techniques, you will need to be familiar with glazes. Adding a glaze to a paint extends its drying time, giving you more flexibility in creating your finish. Glazes also make paint less opaque, giving it a translucent look (the more glaze you add, the more translucent the effect). Glazes come in either oil-based or water-based formulas. Use water-based glazes with water-based paints, and oil-based glazes with oil-based paints.

When working with small objects, you will most likely use artist's acrylic or oil colors, which you can find in an art or craft supply shop. They both come in tubes and are ready to use. Acrylics dry fast, are opaque, and provide good coverage by providing an even-colored coat. They are strong and durable due to their basic composition, which

is similar to modern-day plastics. They're water-based and clean up with soap and water.

Oil colors dry slowly and need to be thinned with linseed oil. Oil colors work very well in techniques where a layered or washed effect is needed; the thicker, opaque acrylics will not work in these instances. You will need turpentine for clean-up after using oil paints.

If you want to mix your own colors, you can use dry pigments. Dry pigments are colors in powder form. When mixed with a liquid medium such as gesso or gloss medium (in either an oil or acrylic base), they impart color to the medium and are ready for application.

Make sure the bole is applied as smoothly as possible, because any brush marks will show through the finished leafed surface. Disposable foam brushes work well for applying the bole, since they don't leave the visible brush strokes you get when using an artist's brush. Allow the bole to dry thoroughly before moving to Step 3.

You may also use spray paints for your base coat. They are useful when working with larger objects. While spray paints are designed to save you time by covering surfaces quickly and easily, they do not give you the accuracy and precision you get with a brush. If you do use spray paint, be careful to apply it in several light layers to avoid drips that will affect the look of the finished gilded surface.

For some projects, the bole can also serve as the sealer coat, thus combining Step 1 and Step 2. The composition of acrylic paints makes them particularly good for sealing some surfaces. But do not attempt this just to save time. Remember, a properly prepared surface will give you the quality results you seek and contribute to the durability of an object. This short-cut is never recommended for raw wood surfaces.

You may decide not to use a bole on some objects you'll be gilding—items that don't need much preparation and are ready to accept the size, or that are already a color you prefer. Just remember that any cracks in the finished leaf will allow the color underneath to show. It's always better to plan ahead by projecting what the object will look like if its original color comes through. If you're not happy with this, you can simply change it by applying the bole before you go any further with your gilding.

Gallery of Gilding

⟩ Gilded Throne

BARBARA BROZIK

42" x 22" x 22"
(106.5 x 56 x 56cm).

far left: Gold, silver, and variegated leaf over acrylic on carved wood with an epoxy resin finish.

left: Detail.

PHOTO: **Bart Kasden**

BESS BAIRD ⟩ Reptile Park

11" x 8" x 9" (28 x 20.5 x 23cm).

Layered acrylic gesso over a balsa wood form; oil-gilded, 22k gold leaf over polymer shapes.

PHOTO: **Evan Bracken**

Step 3: Apply the Size

THE projects in this book use water-based or oil-based size. Both are easy to use for contemporary gilding. There are several commercial preparations available through art and craft supply shops or they may be ordered from a leaf supply company. Size is often called by different names, such as leaf adhesive, leaf sizing, resin size (oil size), or gold leaf size.

If you're unsure whether the size you're buying is oil-based or water-based, open the bottle, observe, and smell. You will know immediately if the size is oil-based, since the size will have an oily, resin smell. Oil-based size is also clear or lightly tinted. If the size is opaque, white, and smells faintly of ammonia or like latex paint, you can be certain the size is water-based. Both oil-based and water-based size are ready to use from the bottle.

Cleaning up after using water-based size is easier because it is water-soluble; warm water and a little soap will do it. With oil-based size, you'll need to clean up with mineral spirits, which now comes in nearly odorless preparations at art, craft, paint, and hardware shops. When you use mineral spirits, you will have to dispose of this solvent in accordance with local regulations.

When using oil-based size and water-based size, follow the procedures for oil gilding: apply the size and wait for it to become tacky before applying the leaf. You know the size is tacky and ready to accept the leaf when it is no longer wet and your finger hesitates as you gently rub it over the surface. Some gilders even claim you can hear when the size is ready because your finger will "whistle" across the surface.

Once the size becomes tacky, or "reaches tack," it will remain tacky for several hours before it dries completely and "loses tack." If this happens, you must repeat the process of applying size and waiting until it becomes tacky again before laying the leaf. Weather can affect the time it takes for any size to become tacky, so take into account humid or dry conditions.

If you apply the leaf when the size is still wet rather than tacky, you'll "drown" the leaf. While the leaf will stick, the wet size will dull the luster of the leaf, and the finished surface will have a rough appearance.

Oil-based size comes in three preparations determined by their different tack times: three-hour, 12-hour and 24-hour. Experienced gilders advise that applying the leaf when the oil-based size has almost lost its tack (when it's almost completely dry) gives the best results. They also believe the size that takes the longest to reach tack creates a better finished product. When you start out, you may want to try the faster drying sizes for quicker results, then later experiment with different sizes until you find a product and a method that match your needs.

Water-based size becomes tacky in 15 to 30 minutes and remains tacky for 36 hours. Most water-based sizes are milky white; some are white with a purple tint. As it dries to tack, water-based size turns clear, a good indication that it is ready to accept the leaf.

It's better to stir the size or gently shake it before application. Vigorous shaking will create bubbles that will pop when the size is applied, creating small craters that will show underneath the leaf and give the surface a rough appearance.

Apply the size as evenly as possible. This is the last application before the leaf goes on, so you want to make sure the surface remains smooth, free from excess brush strokes or drips. Disposable foam brushes work well for this step, but you can also use an artist's brush for applying the size.

Gallery of Gilding

} Treasure Box

LUCINDA CARLSTROM & LESLIE BOAN

24" x 10" x 14" (61 x 25 x 35.5 cm)

Cut and sewn gilded paper applied to a gilded, hinged box. The exterior uses Japanese papers, Japanese antique leaf, bronze leaf, gold leaf, and silk.

PHOTO: **Bart's Art**

SHARON SLOAN } **The Dragon Hold**

9" x 20½" diameter (23 x 52 cm diameter).

Hand-built and wheel-thrown, pit-fired pot with water-gilded copper leaf.

PHOTO: **Evan Bracken**

Step 4: Lay the Leaf

THE LEAF IN ITS BOOK

CUTTING THE BINDING

CUTTING THE LEAF

TRANSFERRING THE LEAF

APPLYING THE LEAF

SMOOTHING THE LEAF

LEAF comes in books, each containing 25 leaves (sheets) of thinly beaten metal. (Photo 1.) Loose leaf is the most common form of packaging and is suitable for all types of gilding. Each leaf is separated by a thin sheet of bound, rouged tissue paper (the rouge in the tissue paper gives it a pale red color and serves to prevent the metal from sticking). Loose leaf can be transferred from the book with a gilder's tip, or it can be handled with the tissue paper that comes in the book.

Transfer leaf, also called patent leaf, is another way of packaging leaf. Like loose leaf, it comes in a bound book. However, each leaf is pressure-applied to a piece of tissue paper. Because leaf is so thin and can easily catch a breeze or a sneeze, transfer leaf is recommended for drafty conditions or for gilding outdoors. Transfer leaf works best on flat surfaces, since the tissue paper backing prevents the leaf from easily settling into the crevices of raised or carved surfaces. Transfer leaf is not suitable for water gilding.

To lay loose leaf, begin by cutting the binding of the book with scissors. (Photo 2.) If you need to cut the sheet into smaller pieces, do so between two pieces of the tissue paper that come in the book. (Photo 3.) You may also use your hands to tear the leaf into smaller sizes between two pieces of tissue paper.

One way to transfer the leaf from its book to an object is to use a gilder's tip. Before picking up the leaf, rub the gilder's tip back and forth over the hair on your head or your arm. The natural oil from your hair combined with any static electricity it generates help the hairs of the gilder's tip grab the leaf. Then move the leaf to the object and gently lay it on the sized surface.

Some gilders take a table knife and gently breathe on it. The moisture from their breath is just enough to pick up the leaf for transfer.

The preferred and easiest way to transfer the leaf is to simply pick it up with your hands, using the tissue paper as a backing. (Photo 4.) This is the favored method of most contemporary gilders. As much as possible, you should avoid touching with your bare hands any leaf that tarnishes. Some gilders apply talcum powder to their hands before laying the leaf, to act as a barrier between bare hands and the thinly beaten metal.

Begin applying the leaf to the tacky surface. Pick up the tissue and leaf and lay the leaf face down on the sized surface. Gently rub the leaf with the tissue paper to help the leaf adhere to the surface. (Photo 5.) Overlap each piece ⅛ inch (3 mm). Work your way from the inside to the outside of an object and from the bottom to the top. If you miss a spot, you can always go back and apply more leaf.

If you are laying transfer leaf, pick up the leaf and the tissue paper to which it has been pressure-applied. Lay the leaf face down on the sized surface. Gently rub the tissue backing to adhere the leaf to the size and then gently remove the tissue paper. Remember that transfer leaf works best on flat surfaces.

When you have laid a section of leaf, use a bob or a brush to smooth the leaf gently into place. (Photo 6.) A bob is a helpful tool that you can make yourself. Cut a square of cotton knit (or silk for finer work) approximately 4 inches (10 cm) square. Place one to three cotton balls in the middle of the fabric, then draw the ends of the square together and secure them close to the cotton balls with a rubber band. The bob should look like a little sack with a tail. A bob is also useful for applying varnish in Step 7. Be aware that laying leaf on a raised or carved surface takes extra patience. You may need more than one layer of leaf to cover the curves, angles, and crevices of these objects. It is best to lay small pieces of leaf at a time when working on these surfaces, moving slowly over the hills and valleys.

Gently tamp the leaf into place, using a brush. A stencil brush, with its thick round shape, seems particularly suited for tamping the leaf into raised areas. If you desire better coverage, resize the surface, wait for it to reach tack, and then apply another layer of leaf.

You may notice that small cracks occur during the leafing process and expose the bole underneath the leaf. You can leave these "faults" if they give you the desired look you want for your project, or you can fill them with skewings—small bits of scrap leaf that are left over from brushing away the excess leaf in Step Five. Carefully pick the skewings up with the tip of a brush (sable works best) and lay them on the small areas you wish to cover. This is known as "faulting."

Once you have laid the leaf on the entire object, allow the leaf to "dry." This expression actually refers to allowing the size to dry and the leaf to "set" on the adhesive. You may want to wait a few hours or even overnight before proceeding to Step Five.

GILDING WITH METALLIC POWDERS

Another method of gilding uses bronze powders, which are metals in powdered form. When you use them, you technically fall within the definition of gilding, since you are applying a skin of metal to a prepared surface.

Bronze powders come in a full range of metallic colors and are used much the same way as dry paint pigments. You can mix them with a medium or binder (paint base) to make your own metallic paint, or you can apply them directly to a sized surface for a process known as *flash gilding*. Bronze powders work particularly well on hard-to-reach surfaces that may be inaccessible for applying leaf.

These powders are very fine. As you work, they can enter your system as you breathe. It is advisable to wear a painter's mask when working with them. If you are going to work with them for any length of time, or if you are working in a confined space, you may need to wear a painter's respirator.

Mica powders are nontoxic, environmentally safe alternatives to bronze powders. They are made from mica platelets that have been coated with titanium dioxide and/or iron oxide. You can get them in virtually all metallic colors and use them the same way as bronze powders.

STEP 5: Brush Excess Leaf From the Surface

WITH a bristle brush, gently remove the excess leaf. Always brush in the direction of the overlap to prevent the leaf from tearing.

You will have small piles of scrap leaf left over from this step. Do not throw them away. These are called skewings and they are invaluable for filling small faults or holidays. Save the skewings of each leaf you use in separate small boxes or bags for future use.

Once you brush away the excess, check the surface for any cracks or separations in the leaf. Repair them if desired by applying the skewings with a sable brush. You may need to resize an area if it is no longer tacky to the touch.

SALLY BRYENTON } **Re-Mem-Member**

13½" x 10" (34 x 25 cm) Mixed media with sculpted, gilded head.
PHOTO: **Evan Bracken**

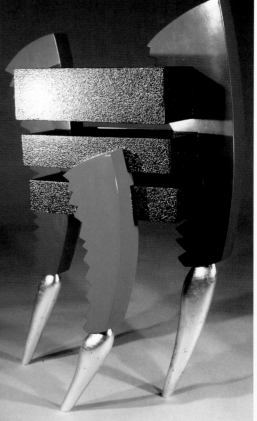

⁞ Sawtooth Tango

BRENT SKIDMORE

40" x 24" x 12" (101.5 x 61 x 30.5 cm)

Silver composition leaf, enamel base coat, and gesso primer over birch plywood, pear, and poplar wood.

PHOTO: **Brent Skidmore**

Step 6: Distress, Antique, or Decorate the Leaf

AFTER the leaf has been laid, you can alter or enhance the gilded surface for a multitude of special effects. This step is optional and depends on your concept of the finished project. You can make the leaf look older, tone down the color, overpaint it, or add surface decorations. The easiest way to get an antique look is to leave the faults that show the bole underneath the leaf, or you can intentionally create cracks as you lay the leaf.

You may want to look in your paint store for commercial preparations for antiquing or other effects. You can find products that create a copper verdigris finish, for instance. There are also antique glazes or mediums available at craft supply shops. You can find a crackle varnish in paint or craft supply stores which produces the results its name implies; when applied, it creates a crackled surface.

Artist's oil colors can be used to shade areas of your surface for an antique effect. Use a rag to apply the color where you want it on the gilded surface (in the faults, for instance), then wipe off the excess. You may want to thin the paint with linseed oil before application for a more transparent color. You can clean artist's oil colors with turpentine. Burnt umber or raw sienna oil colors work best for an antique finish, but you can use any color you desire.

Do not use acrylic artist's paints for this technique; they are opaque and will not give you the "washed" effect that you will get from oil paints. Allow the oil paints to dry thoroughly before applying a sealer coat of varnish.

Another way to antique a surface it is to use wood wiping stains. These oil-based stains come in a variety of wood tones and are available at paint or hardware stores. Use a rag to apply the stain to your gilded surface, then wipe off the excess. To clean up after using these stains, you will need to use mineral spirits. Do not use penetrating wood stains for this technique; they are made to stain raw wood by penetrating the wood fibers and are not meant for use on finished surfaces.

A traditional way to distress or antique a gilded surface involves the use of rottenstone, or ground limestone, which is readily available in paint or hardware stores. Its dusty grey color can immediately make an object look older. For application on leaf, mix the rottenstone with paste wax (a thick wax packed in cans and used for protecting furniture and floors) to the desired color. Then apply the mixture to the gilded surface with a rag until you achieve the desired results.

Decoupage medium is handy for fixing a print or decorative paper to a surface. It is a water-based formula found in art or craft supply stores. Unlike glue, you do not apply it to the reverse side of the object you wish to attach. Instead, you lay the print or paper face up on the surface; then, using a brush, you apply the decoupage medium like paint to both the paper and the surface. The medium seals the paper to the surface, effectively gluing them together.

Another short-cut for gluing is spray adhesive, which you can find in art or craft supply shops. It dries quickly and is suitable only for light gluing jobs; it's ideal for working with paper.

Gallery of Gilding

RANDY SHULL ≷ Midas

80" x 30" x 10" (200 x 76 x 25 cm)

While the laminated wood surface is painted with metallic acrylic paints, the look of the piece and its approach replicate a fine leafed surface.

PHOTO: **Martin Fox**

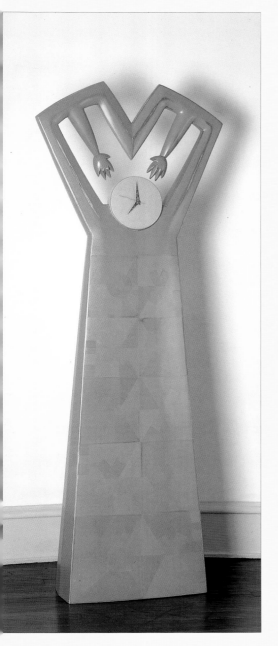

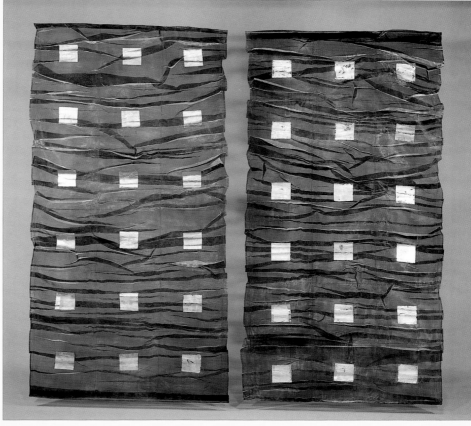

JUNCO SATO POLLACK ≷ Rimpa

above: Genuine gold and silver leaf with heat-transferred aluminum on polyester and silk.

right: Detail.

Step 7: Seal the Surface

IF **YOU** are using a leaf that tarnishes (composition leaf, silver leaf, variegated leaf, or copper leaf), you must seal the gilded surface. You do not need to seal real gold leaf, because it will not tarnish. However, if you want extra protection for a real gold surface, you may decide to apply a protective sealer coat.

The best protective coat for a gilded surface is varnish. It comes in either oil-based or water-based preparations that you apply with a brush. Both come in matte, satin, and gloss finishes (matte has no shine, satin a moderate shine, gloss is the shiniest).

You can clean water-based varnish with soap and water. Oil varnish needs to be cleaned with mineral spirits. Water-based varnish is easier to use, but oil varnish provides a more durable finish.

Shellac can be used for a sealer coat but may alter the color of the leaf. You can also use acrylic spray sealers (also referred to as spray fixatives and lacquers) found in art and craft supply shops. These provide very light protection and are not suitable for objects that will get much wear. Spray sealers are ideal for paper projects.

Gallery of Gilding

LAURIE GODDARD } **Patinated Bowls**

9" and 14" (23 and 35.5 cm) diameters. Turned wooden bowls gilded with composition leaf that is chemically "patinated" to create the colors and effects. PHOTO: **Evan Bracken**

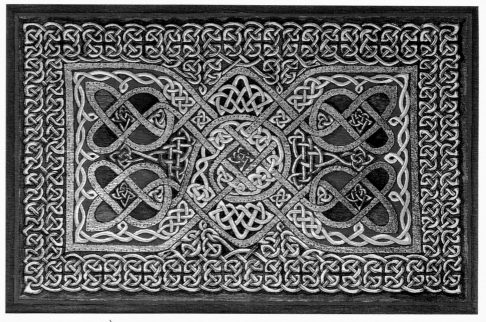

GRACE BAGGOT 〉 **Noble Sea**

15½" x 13" (39 x 33 cm). Watercolor enhanced with gold leaf.   PHOTO: **Evan Bracken**

JANET HANCHEY 〉 **Candlemas**

18" x 20" (45.5 x 51 cm)
Oil-painted panel with oil-gilded gold leaf.

Frames

DESIGNER } **Grace Baggot**

Small Oval Frame

This project unites the latest technology with an ancient craft for a look that is timeless in its appeal. While you will know that the up-to-date injection-molded foam frame is inexpensive and lightweight, the antiqued gold surface will make others think twice about the frame's origin.

MATERIALS

Injection-molded foam frame
Denatured alcohol
Resin (oil) size
Transfer gold leaf
Yellow ocher and raw umber casein-based
  paints*

* Casein is produced from sour skim milk. It is used as a glue or as a binder (base) for pigments and is available at art supply stores.

TOOLS

Soft, lint-free rags
Natural hair brush
Stipple brush

INSTRUCTIONS

1. Clean the frame's surface with a rag and denatured alcohol.

2. Apply the resin (oil) size with a brush.

3. Allow the size to reach tack. Apply the transfer leaf.

4. Allow the leaf to dry overnight.

5. Remove the excess leaf by gently brushing the surface.

6. Apply the yellow ocher casein to the raised leafed surface to fill and hide the "holidays."

7. Wipe off the excess casein with a soft rag.

8. Darken the yellow ocher casein by mixing it with the raw umber casein until you are pleased with the color. Using the stipple brush, apply the casein to the surface where you want to simulate dirt. Using a soft rag, gently dab off the excess casein.

9. You can achieve variations in the toning depending on the amount of casein you apply; the more you apply, the older the frame will appear.

Free-Standing Mat Frame

Quick, simple, and elegant. This frame's contemporary outlook will graciously highlight any photo.

MATERIALS

Double picture mat with back board

Matte finish spray paint in the colors of your choice

Water-based leaf adhesive

Composition gold leaf

White glue or glue gun and glue sticks

Wax paper

Easel backing

2-inch (5 cm) packing tape

TOOLS

Cellulose sponge

Small dish

Scissors

Soft artist's brush

INSTRUCTIONS

1. If the mat is not the desired color, spray it with matte finish paint in the color of your choice.

2. Pour some size in a small dish. Cut a long, thin strip from a cellulose sponge. Dip this strip into the size.

3. Randomly sponge the size onto the top layer of the double mat. Allow the size to reach tack.

4. Using either new pieces of gold leaf or skewings, apply leaf to the sized areas of the mat. Press the leaf onto the mat with a piece of the tissue paper that comes with the leaf. Brush off the excess leaf with a soft artist's brush.

5. Glue the second layer of the mat to the back of the gilded top layer using either white glue or a glue gun and glue sticks. If you are using white glue, place a piece of wax paper over the glued layers, then lay heavy books on top of that. The wax paper will protect the layers while the books help the layers dry flat. Allow the glue to dry thoroughly.

6. Glue the easel back to the back board of the mat using either white glue or a glue gun and glue sticks. Again, if you're using white glue, use the wax paper over the glued layers and press the layers between heavy books until the glue dries thoroughly.

7. To hinge the back board to the mat, first turn the mat over with the gilded side facing down. Turn the back board over so the easel is facing down. Place the inside top of the back board flush to the inside top of the mat. Take a 3-inch (7.5 cm) length of packing tape and fold the tape in half, sticky side out. Position the tape at the center back of the mat. Stick half of the tape to the mat and half of the tape to the back board.

DESIGNER } **Laura Sims**

Icon and Relief

There's a certain satisfaction in making an instant antique from today's readily available materials. These easily constructed frames allow you to achieve collector status in no time.

Icon (top)

MATERIALS

Print
Spray acrylic sealer
Door-stop molding*
Small finishing nails (brads)
Wood filler
¼ inch (.5 cm) plywood
Sanding sealer
White acrylic gesso tinted with
 Venetian red dry paint pigment
Decoupage medium**
Marbleized paper
Leaf size
Composition gold leaf
Burnt umber water-based
 antiquing medium**
White glue
Braiding
Picture wire

* Door-stop molding is available in home-improvement stores, and at lumber yards.

** You can find these in craft supply shops.

TOOLS

Tape measure
Miter box
Saw
Hammer
Sandpaper
Paint brushes
Disposable foam brushes
Artist's brushes
Soft, lint-free rags

INSTRUCTIONS

1. Find a print that you like and photo copy it in color. This makes the print look older. Spray the front and back of the photo-copied print with acrylic sealer.

2. Measure the print to determine the size of the frame.

3. Using the saw and miter box, cut the molding for the frame according to the dimensions of the print. Assemble the frame, using the hammer and the small finishing nails. Fill any nail holes with wood filler, allow to dry, then sand the frame.

4. Cut a backing for the print to fit the frame from the ¼ inch (.5 cm) plywood.

5. Apply a coat of sanding sealer to the frame and the plywood backing.

6. Mix the Venetian red pigment into the white gesso until the gesso is lightly colored. Apply two or three coats of this tinted gesso to the frame and backing. Allow each coat to dry thoroughly, sanding each coat before applying the next. Allow to dry.

7. Position the print on the center of the backing. Using a brush, apply the decoupage medium over the print and plywood backing. The decoupage medium will seal the print in place, effectively gluing it to the board.

8. Cut strips of the marbleized paper large enough to cover the flat surfaces of the door-stop molding. Place the paper on the frame's flat surfaces. Using a brush, apply the decoupage medium over the paper, fixing the paper to the frame. Allow to dry.

9. Apply the leaf size to the remaining surfaces with a disposable foam brush. Wait for it to reach tack, then apply the composition leaf. Let the leaf dry thoroughly before brushing off the excess leaf.

10. Spray on a coat of acrylic sealer. Allow to dry.

11. Apply a coat of the burnt umber water-based antiquing medium. Using a soft rag, wipe off the antiquing medium until you get the results you desire. More medium will make the frame look older and darker; less medium will impart a mellow tone to the gold.

12. Attach the backing board to the frame and secure it with the small nails. You can also use white glue to attach it.

13. If you feel the print needs it for aesthetic reasons, attach a thin strip of braiding or other thin material (like painted balsa wood) around the print with white glue .

14. Spray the entire icon with acrylic sealer.

15. Attach a hanging wire to the back of the frame.

DESIGNER } **Fred Gaylor**

Relief (bottom)

MATERIALS

Cast relief *

One frame approximately
  11 x 12 x 1½ inches
  (28 x 30.5 x 4cm)

One frame approximately
  7 x 8 x 1½ inches
  (18 x 20.5 x 4cm)

Sanding sealer or clear
  shellac

Leaf size

Copper leaf

Burnt umber and raw
  umber water-based glaze

Composition gold leaf

Decorative paper

Decoupage medium

Composition gold leaf

Small nails

Spray acrylic sealer

Picture hanging hardware

** This relief was originally cast in concrete. You may be able to find
similar reliefs cast in plaster at craft supply shops.*

TOOLS

Paint brush for applying
  sealer or shellac

Nut pick or other sharp,
  pointed tool

Brushes for applying size
  and decoupage medium

Stencil brush

Soft, lint-free rags

Scissors

Small hammer

Hot glue gun and glue
  sticks

INSTRUCTIONS

1. Clean the relief and seal it with sanding sealer or
clear shellac.

2. Apply the leaf size to the relief. Allow it to become
tacky, then apply the copper leaf. Use a nut pick or other
similar pointed tool to gently work the leaf into the
crevices of the relief.

3. Use a stencil brush to further tamp the leaf into the crevices. Then, using the same brush, gently brush off the excess leaf. Allow to dry.

4. Mix burnt umber and raw umber antiquing mediums together until you get a color you prefer. Apply the medium to the copper-leafed relief using a soft rag. With a clean, soft rag, wipe off some of the medium, leaving more in the crevices of the relief. Allow to dry.

5. Apply a coat of spray acrylic sealer to the relief. Allow to dry.

6. Apply the leaf size to the larger frame, wait for it to become tacky, then apply the copper leaf. When dry, apply the antiquing medium, following the same procedure as in Step 4. Allow to dry.

7. Cut strips of decorative paper large enough to cover the inside of the large frame. Position the paper where you want it on the frame. Using a brush, apply the decoupage medium over the paper on the frame. This seals the paper in place. Allow to dry.

8. Apply gold composition leaf and antiquing medium to the small frame following the instructions in Step 6.

9. Place the relief in the smaller frame, then position the smaller frame inside the larger frame. Attach the frames to each other using small nails or hot glue.

10. Spray the entire piece with acrylic sealer.

11. Attach the picture-hanging hardware to the back of the frame.

Round Frame With Floral Decoration

The designer purchased this frame at a yard sale for less money than it takes to buy a cup of cappuccino. It is truly a testament to the transformative magic of the gilder's craft.

MATERIALS

One book of 23-karat loose gold leaf

12-hour oil size

Yellow sandable auto body spray primer (lacquer base)

TOOLS

1-inch (2.5 cm) gilder's tip

3-inch (7.5 cm) gilder's tip

1-inch (2.5 cm) ox hair mop brush

#8 French stipple brush (big, round, bristle brush with a flat head)

Elephant ear sponge (available in ceramic supply stores)

1-inch (2.5 cm) soft, sable or squirrel hair brush

Fine sandpaper

DESIGNER **Margery Sherrill**

INSTRUCTIONS

1. The surface of this frame was in good condition; others that you purchase might not be. If necessary, sand with a fine sandpaper and fill in any holes with wood filler. Sand again, paying particular attention to the areas where you applied the filler. You want to make the surface as smooth as possible before applying the primer.

2. Spray the primer on the frame. Allow to dry. Yellow was chosen as a base coat/primer to help minimize the "faults," the tiny cracks that happen when gilding. When there are carved details like the ones on this frame, there will be more faulting than on a flat surface.

3. Sand the primer coat.

4. Using the ox hair mop, apply the size over the sanded primer. To make sure it covers completely, work the size in different directions.

5. Wait 12 hours or until the size is ready to accept the gold. You will need to cut the leaf into smaller sizes for gilding the carved details. Lay the gold, using the different size gilder's tips as needed.

6. Let the piece sit for 24 hours.

7. Using a clean, soft, sable brush, remove the excess leaf. When all the skewings have been removed, use the elephant ear sponge to gently clean the surface. Wet the sponge, then ring out any remaining moisture with a towel until it is barely damp. Wait two days.

8. Using the French stipple brush, gently brush the surface. This reduces the reflective shine of the leaf and gives rich depth to the gold.

Triptych

Triptychs contain portraits of saints and deities and are used as portable altars for private worship. The richness of gold and depth of copper provide shimmering surroundings for this depiction of Saint Elizabeth.

DESIGNER } **Fred Gaylor**

MATERIALS

Smooth finished plywood

Sanding sealer

Acrylic gesso tinted with red oxide
   dry paint pigment

An image for the triptych (this can
   be a photo, a print, or picture cut
   from a greeting card or magazine)

Spray acrylic sealer

White glue

Cardboard

Leaf size

Transfer composition gold leaf

Transfer copper leaf

Fabric

Powdered graphite

Four small hinges

Small latch (optional)

TOOLS

Fine-toothed saw

Brushes for applying sealers
   and paint

Sandpaper

Soft, lint-free rags

Small hard roller (a brayer,
   used in print making, is ideal
   and is available at art and craft
   supply shops)

Scissors

Craft knife

Brush for applying size

Spoon

Screwdriver

INSTRUCTIONS

1. Cut two rounded arched panels from the smooth-finished plywood.

2. Using a fine-toothed saw, cut one of the rounded arched panels down the middle to form the two side panels.

3. Apply the sanding sealer. Allow to dry.

4. Mix red oxide dry paint pigment into white acrylic gesso until it is the color you desire. Apply two or three coats of this gesso to the panel, sanding it smooth after each coat.

5. Seal the image you'll be using with spray acrylic sealer.

6. Apply the image to the center panel with white glue. Take a damp rag and press the image to the wood. Use a small roller (brayer) to eliminate any wrinkles.

7. Use the cardboard to create a border for the image. Cut the board in ¼ inch (.5 cm) strips. Lay the cardboard around the edges of the image and glue with white glue.

8. Apply the size to one side and the outer edges of each panel. Also size the cardboard on the center panel that surrounds the image. Allow the size to reach tack.

9. Apply the transfer gold and copper leaf. Do this by laying the leaf face-down on the sized surface. Use a slightly damp cloth to moisten the backing paper of the transfer leaf. Then, take the smooth side of a spoon and rub it over the paper to transfer the leaf onto the surface. Alternate gold and copper in the areas you desire. Allow some of the red undercoating to show through. (Any wood grain that shows contributes to the aged look.)

10. Glue the fabric to the outside surface of the panels. You can enhance the overall design by selecting a fabric that has a medieval look in colors that coordinate with the colors of the image.

11. Take the hinges and hinge the center and side panels together. To make the hinges look older, apply leaf size to the hinges, allow it to reach tack, and then rub powdered graphite on them. This will make them look like lead or time-worn metal.

12. If you desire, you can also place a small latch on the outside of the front panels for closing the triptych.

DESIGNER } **LAURA SIMS**

Bookmarks

Gold marks the spot. Are you tired of those dog-eared pages and wispy slips of paper? It's easy to remember just where you left off with your reading when a glint of gold catches your eye.

MATERIALS

Heavy (60 lb) cardstock in the colors of your choice

Metallic gold and metallic copper acrylic paint

Decorative paper

White glue

Wax paper

Water-based leaf adhesive

Composition gold leaf

Leaf sealer (varnish)

TOOLS

Scissors

Cellulose sponge

Two artist's brushes between sizes #2 and #8

INSTRUCTIONS

1. Cut a rectangle from the cardstock approximately 2 inches x 8½ inches (5 x 22 cm).

2. Cut a small piece from the cellulose sponge. Dip the sponge in the metallic gold paint. Gently blot the edges of the rectangle with the sponge. Allow to dry. Repeat with the metallic copper paint. Set aside to dry.

3. Cut two rectangles of decorative paper ½ inch (1.5 cm) smaller in both directions than the first rectangle—that is, 1½ inches x 8 inches (4 x 20.5 cm).

4. Brush a thin coat of white glue on the back of one of the smaller rectangles. Center it on the larger rectangle and stick them together.

5. Place the glued rectangles on a flat surface and lay a piece of wax paper over them. Lay a heavy book on top of the rectangles and wax paper until the glue dries.

6. Gild the second small rectangle by applying leaf size to the rectangle, waiting for the size to reach tack, then applying composition gold leaf. Brush off excess leaf.

7. Tear a strip from the center of the gilded rectangle. The more uneven the tear, the better the look of the finished bookmark.

8. With a brush, seal the leaf with leaf sealer and allow to dry.

9. Line up the straight edges of the torn paper with the straight edges of the small rectangle. The uneven edges should be on the inside,

allowing the decorative paper to show through. Glue the torn paper to the decorative-paper rectangle. Cover the bookmark with wax paper and lay a heavy book on top of the bookmark and wax paper until the glue dries.

Variation

1. Cut a rectangle from the cardstock approximately 2 inches x 8½ inches (5 x 22 cm).

2. Following Step 2 in the above instructions, sponge-paint the edges of the rectangle.

3. Cut pieces of cardstock into decorative shapes, then gild and seal them.

4. Cut the decorative paper in shapes that duplicate the shapes of the gilded stock, only smaller.

5. Glue the gilded shape to the sponged rectangle, then glue the cut decorative paper to the gilded cardstock.

6. Cover the bookmark with wax paper, and lay a heavy book on top of the bookmark and wax paper until the glue dries.

Paper

DESIGNER } Terry Taylor

Relief Cartouche Cards

A cartouche is an architectural ornament, an embellishment that enhances the functional with a measure of grace. The decorative touches added to these cards make them an elegant framework for expressing your personal sentiments to family and friends.

MATERIALS

Blank greeting cards and envelopes

Small scraps of cardboard or mat board

White glue

Clear matte acrylic spray

Water-based size

Composition leaf (gold, silver, or copper)

Spray adhesive

Assorted beads, embroidery thread, pictures to collage (optional)

TOOLS

Scissors

Craft knife

INSTRUCTIONS

1. Determine the size of the relief you'll attach to the card. The card shown has a 2-inch x 3-inch (5 x 7.5 cm) relief, which is a good size in proportion to the card. Cut a piece of mat board 2 inches x 3 inches in size.

2. Cut small pieces of cardboard to attach to the mat board to create the relief. The surface can be covered with geometric designs or specific designs for various holidays (such as stars, hearts, trees, leaf forms, etc.). Use white glue to attach these pieces to the mat board. Allow to dry.

3. When dry, give the relief a light coat of clear matte acrylic spray to serve as a sealer coat.

4. You may gild your relief in two ways. Use the traditional method of applying size and leaf. Or spray the relief with spray adhesive, allow to dry until tacky and then apply the leaf.

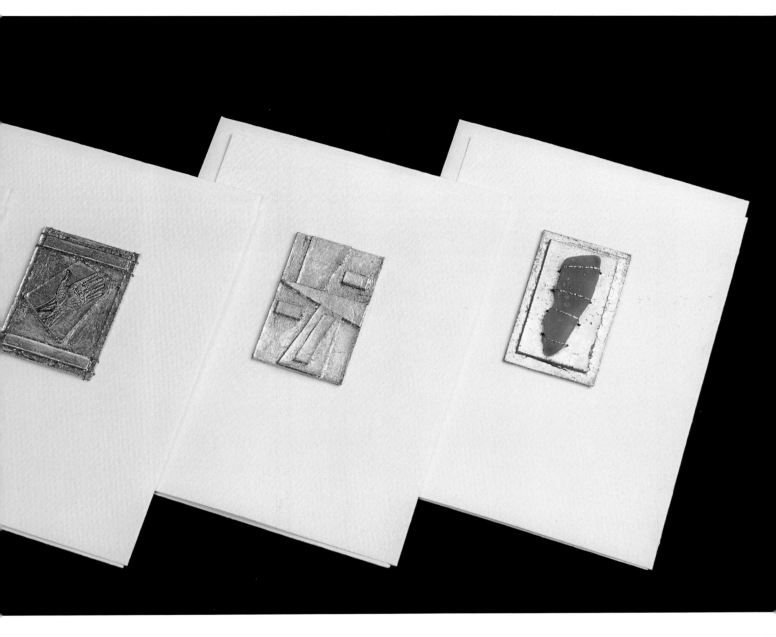

5. When the relief is gilded, you may add pictures to the card for a collaged effect (such as the hand or the small photograph shown). Simply attach them with the white glue and allow to dry.

6. Seal the gilded relief with clear matte acrylic spray.

7. Use white glue to attach the relief to the card.

8. You may further enhance the relief with embroidery threads and beads if desired.

Gilded Origami Paper Collage

Now you can enjoy a swarm of golden butterflies throughout the year.
If you create your own from decorative papers and composition leaf, you
can relive memories of your favorite sun-dappled spring.

Laura Sims

MATERIALS

Solid and printed decorative papers
Heavyweight white cardboard
White glue
Water-based leaf adhesive
Composition gold leaf
Tissue paper
Shadow box frame

TOOLS

Two artist's brushes between the sizes #2 and #8
Rolling pin

INSTRUCTIONS

1. Create a desired collage background, using a combination of the solid and printed decorative papers. Cut or tear papers in desired shapes. Arrange them to your liking on a piece of heavy white cardboard and glue them in place using white glue.

2. Gild the back of a large piece of decorative paper. Begin by laying the paper on a flat surface.

3. Brush the size onto the paper and let it achieve tack.

4. Using the tissue paper that comes with the composition gold leaf, gently pick up a sheet of leaf and carefully place it in the upper corner of the sized paper. Pick up the next sheet of leaf and barely overlap the edge of the previous sheet. Continue until the large piece of paper is completely gilded.

5. Lay a large piece of tissue paper over the completely gilded sheet and firmly press the gold leaf, first using your fingers, then using a rolling pin.

6. Cut the gilded paper into squares ranging from large to small.

7. Fold the squares into origami butterflies following the instructions on the next page.

8. Arrange the folded butterflies on the collaged background and glue them in place. To create an illusion of depth, place the larger butterflies in one of the lower corners and graduate to the smallest butterflies in the upper diagonal corner.

9. Frame in a shadow box frame.

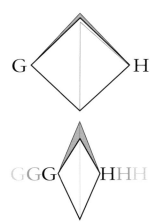

Origami Butterfly

*There are many patterns for origami
butterflies. You can use this
one to get started, then investigate
others that might suit your fancy.
Fold the butterflies with the decorative
paper on the outside. This allows the gold to
peek out from inside the butterflies, making them
look like they've caught the sun on their wings.*

1. Begin with the
paper gold-side-up.
Fold the paper
diagonally, bringing
point A to point B.

A

B

2. Fold the paper again, bringing point C to point D.

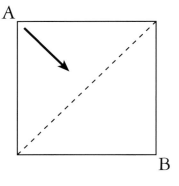

C

D

C-D

3. Turn the paper over and bring point E to point F.

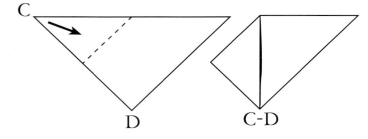

E

F

E-F

4. Turn the paper over so
the open edges are on top.
Pick the paper up, grasping
it by points G and H.
Gently push points G and
H together; the paper will
open as you do so. Bring
point G to point H and
crease the paper.

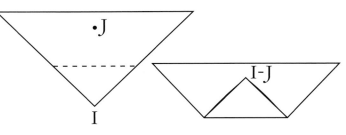

G

H

GGG

HHH

5. Fold point I up to point J.

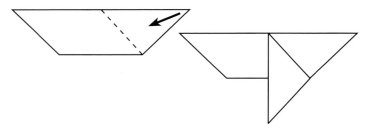

•J

I

I-J

6. Turn the paper over. Starting on the right side,
fold the top layer of the paper down along the
indicated fold line.

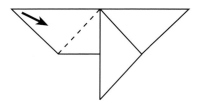

7. Do the same on the
left side, folding the top
layer down on the
indicated fold line.

8. The finished butterfly
will look like this.

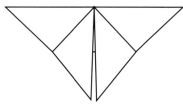

Books

Encase your golden thoughts in these gilded books. With a little leaf and some decorative papers, plain book covers gain a sparkling exterior. This is a perfect treatment for making a journal as much of a personal statement without as within.

DESIGNER **Susan Lightcap**

MATERIALS

Book with plain cover

Assorted decorative/handmade papers

Matte spray fixative

White glue

Water-based size

Composition gold leaf or real gold leaf

TOOLS

Pencil with eraser

Scissors

Brushes for applying glue and size

Teaspoon

Sea sponge

Saucer

Blunt, thin-edged table knife

1-inch (2.5 cm) bristle brush for tamping leaf and removing excess

INSTRUCTIONS

1. Make sure that the surface of the book is clean and free of dirt or grease.

2. Draw the shapes of your choice on the decorative papers, then cut or tear them out.

3. Spray the shapes with matte fixative (to seal the surface of the paper so the gilding size won't soak in). Allow to dry.

4. Using the brush, apply the white glue sparingly to the book cover, then glue on the shapes.

5. With the rounded back of the teaspoon, gently press the shapes onto the cover, then smooth them. Allow the glue to dry.

6. Gently shake or stir the size until it is thoroughly mixed. Pour a small amount into the saucer.

7. Dip the sea sponge lightly into the gilding size and dab gently onto the collaged book cover. Allow the size to become tacky.

8. Using the table knife, gently lift and position the leaf sheet over the area to be gilded. Take your time and be very careful with the fragile leaf. (Take a deep breath and exhale before this step!)

9. Gently "pound" (tamp) the bristles of the paint brush over the area where you applied the leaf. Light pressure is preferable; the gold leaf will adhere easily to the sticky size. Blow away any extra gold leaf, then use the brush to whisk away any remaining bits.

10. If you are using composition gold leaf, spray the gilded areas with matte spray fixative as a sealer coat.

DESIGNER ⟩ **Laura Sims**

Stationery

*Imagine receiving a letter on stationery accented with gold.
Not only does it provide the perfect setting for a message to
a special person, it is also an inspiration to the letter writer.*

MATERIALS

Paper

Envelopes

Water-based leaf adhesive

Composition gold leaf

TOOLS

Scissors

Small disposable foam brush

Two pure bristle artist's brushes
  between sizes #2 and #8

INSTRUCTIONS

Checkerboard Pattern

1. To make a square stamp for creating the checkerboard, take the scissors and cut off the bevelled end of the foam brush at the bevel line. Then, cut an additional ½ inch (1.5 cm) off the top of the brush.

2. Dip the end of the stamp in the size and sponge a checkerboard pattern along the long edge of the paper and along the short edge of the envelope.

3. Allow the adhesive to turn from milky white to clear and become tacky to the touch.

4. Cut the leaf into a rectangle the width of the checkerboard pattern. Do this by cutting the leaf between two pieces of the tissue paper that come with the leaf.

5. Keeping the cut gold leaf rectangle between the two pieces of tissue paper, lay them on a flat surface. Carefully remove the top piece of tissue paper.

6. Position the stationery adhesive-side-down on the exposed gold leaf.

7. Apply pressure to the back of the stationery by rubbing your finger over the leaf area.

8. Turn the stationery over and remove the excess composition leaf with a soft, dry artist's brush.

9. Repeat Steps 4 through 8 for the envelope.

Intersecting Line Pattern

1. Use a brush to apply the adhesive in the line pattern on the paper and envelope.

2. Allow the adhesive to turn from milky white to clear and become tacky to the touch.

3. Cut the leaf into strips that are wider than the lines of the pattern. Do this by cutting the leaf between two pieces of the tissue paper that come with the leaf.

4. Apply the leaf to the sized areas, pressing the leaf gently with the tissue paper.

Brushed Edge Pattern

1. Use a small artist's brush to paint the adhesive on the stationery. Use short brush strokes while moving down the long edge of the paper, creating a 1-inch (2.5 cm) strip with an uneven edge. Repeat along the short end of the envelope.

2. Allow the adhesive to turn from milky white to clear and become tacky to the touch.

3. Cut the leaf into a strip that is wider than the line of the pattern. Do this by cutting the leaf between two pieces of tissue paper that come with the leaf.

4. Apply the leaf to the sized areas, pressing the leaf gently with the tissue paper.

NOTE: If you need to lift a sheet of composition leaf from its book, take a table knife and breathe on the blade. Then touch the blade to the top of the leaf and lift. The dampness from your breath is enough to "grab" the leaf without damaging it.

Trinket Boxes

DESIGNER } **Kathleen Burke**

All of these started out as small, unfinished wooden boxes from a craft supply shop. They are known as stamp boxes and trinket boxes, names that undeniably define their use. They are also called faerie boxes, which, given their diminutive size, leaves their usage totally to your imagination.

MATERIALS

Small, unfinished wooden boxes

Clear shellac

Acrylic paints in various colors

Gloss urethane varnish

Leaf size

Copper leaf

Composition gold leaf

Silver leaf

Skewings

Commercial preparation that duplicates copper patina*

TOOLS

Fine sandpaper

Artist's brushes for applying paint and size

Camel hair brush for tamping leaf

Chamois

Toothbrush

Small sea sponge

* Optional, depending on your chosen design. Various preparations can be purchased in a paint store or craft supply shop.

BASIC INSTRUCTIONS FOR ALL BOXES

1. Sand the box and seal it with two coats of clear shellac.

2. Apply two coats of acrylic paint in an appropriate color as the base coat for your project.

3. Seal with one coat of clear shellac.

4. On either the outside or inside of the box, paint to achieve your chosen effect according to your design (see individual instructions). Allow to dry.

5. Apply two coats of gloss urethane to the painted portion of the box.

6. Using a small brush, carefully apply the leaf size and let it dry to the proper tack.

7. Apply the leaf and tamp it down with a camel hair brush. Allow the leaf to dry overnight.

8. Brush off the excess leaf and lightly burnish by rubbing the surface gently with a chamois.

9. Seal the entire box with two coats of gloss urethane.

NOTES ON INDIVIDUAL DESIGNS

Red/Copper

Follow Steps 1 through 3 of the basic instructions, using a medium red acrylic paint for the base coat. Allow to dry. Dip the bristles of the toothbrush in black acrylic paint. Hold the toothbrush, bristle side up, close to the surface of the box. Run your thumb over the bristles of the brush. Allow to dry. Then repeat the process, using a metallic gold paint. Use copper leaf on the inside of the box, following Steps 6 through 9 of the basic instructions.

Blue/Variegated Gold

Follow Steps 1 through 3 of the basic instructions, using a phthalo blue acrylic paint for the base coat. ("Phthalo" is short for *phthalocyanine*, a blue-green pigment used in artist's colors.) On the exterior, use a small sea sponge to dab first white, then phthalo green paint. Use variegated leaf on the inside of the box, following Steps 6 through 9 of the basic instructions.

Silver and Gold/White

This is a great way to use your skewings from other projects. Follow Steps 1 through 3 of the basic instructions, using a white acrylic paint for the base coat. Next, apply the size and wait for it to reach the proper tack. Pick up the gold skewings with a camel hair brush and apply randomly over the box and lid, leaving space for the silver skewings. Then pick up the silver skewings with the camel hair brush and apply until the entire piece is covered. Brush off the excess leaf and seal with two coats of gloss urethane.

Variegated Gold/Green Glaze

Follow Steps 1 through 3 of the basic instructions, using a metallic gold acrylic paint for the base coat. On the exterior, gild with gold composition leaf. Paint the inside with several thin glaze coats of phthalo green and white paint over the metallic gold base coat. Seal with two coats of gloss urethane.

Antique Copper/Copper Leaf

Follow Steps 1 through 3 in the basic instructions, using a metallic copper acrylic paint for the base coat. On the outside, use a commercial preparation for duplicating copper patina. Follow the manufacturer's instructions. On the inside of the box, apply copper leaf, following Steps 6 through 9 of the basic instructions.

Anniversary Box

This box was made by designer Happy Veirs as a present to her husband on the occasion of their 50th wedding anniversary. She selected the oriental print for its depiction of a man and woman sailing along life's way.

By using 23 karat gold skewings saved from other projects, she was able to achieve the subtle mottled effect on the gilded portions.

MATERIALS

Small wooden box
Clear shellac
Red acrylic paint
Resin (oil) varnish
Talcum powder
Leaf size
Gold leaf
Print for decoupage
Clear acrylic spray coat
White glue
Mother of pearl (available as flat sheets in art and craft supply shops)
Permanent black marker
High-gloss varnish
Satin-finish varnish
Clear wood wax

TOOLS

Brushes for applying shellac and varnish
Artist's brush for applying paint
#200, #400, and #600 sandpaper
Silk bob
1-inch (2.5 cm) sable brush
Scissors
Craft knife
Soft cloth

INSTRUCTIONS

1. Seal the wood by applying two coats of clear shellac to the interior and exterior of the box. Allow to dry.

2. Sand with the #200 sandpaper until smooth.

3. Apply two coats of red paint to the box. Allow to dry.

4. Apply one coat of resin (oil) varnish. Allow to dry.

5. Using the #400 and #600 sandpaper, sand the box until smooth.

6. Apply the leaf size with a silk bob.

7. Let dry until the size is tacky to the touch (30 to 45 minutes).

8. Powder your hands with the talcum powder. (Avoid touching the leaf with your bare hands.)

9. Apply the gold leaf.

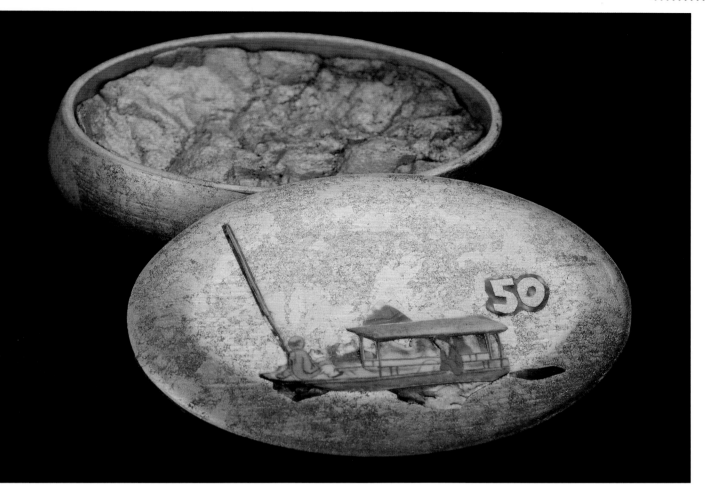

DESIGNER

Happy Veirs

10. Smooth the leaf with a very soft brush or use the rouge paper that comes with the gold leaf.

11. Allow the leaf to dry thoroughly.

12. Seal the box with the varnish and let dry.

13. Cut out the print and glue it on the box with white glue.

14. The mountain and water are mother of pearl. Cut the shapes using a sharp craft knife. To achieve the beautiful colors from the mother of pearl, use a black permanent marker to color the backside of the pearl. Let it dry, then glue the mother of pearl to the box with white glue.

15. Clean up any glue drips with a damp paper towel until all glue is removed.

16. Apply several coats of the high-gloss varnish, allowing each coat to dry thoroughly before applying the next one, then sand with the #600 sandpaper. For this project, 20 coats of satin varnish were applied then sanded.

17. Apply two coats of satin varnish. Allow the first coat to dry thoroughly before applying the second, then sand with the #600 sandpaper.

18. Wax and polish the box with a soft cloth for the final finish.

NOTE: Because the box was made to hold a small piece of jewelry, the interior was fitted with cotton batting that had been sprayed with gold spray paint to blend with the box.

DESIGNER } **Kathleen Burke**

Malachite and Gold Jewelry Chest

Designer Kathleen Burke found this chest in an antique store. She was attracted by its form but disliked the plain, brown, veneered finish. Her remedy was to combine the beauty of deep green malachite, recreated in a faux finish, with the luster of gold.

MATERIALS

Dark green and medium green acrylic paints

Clear shellac

Leaf size

Composition gold leaf

Orange shellac

Gloss urethane

TOOLS

Fine sandpaper

Small angled brush

Rags

Brush for applying size

Camel hair brush

Chamois

INSTRUCTIONS

1. Sand the top of the chest with a fine sandpaper.

2. Using the acrylic paint and the small angled brush, paint the top in a faux malachite pattern. Begin by applying a coat of dark green acrylic paint. Do not allow it to dry before proceeding with the next step. Rinse the brush, then wipe it dry with a clean rag. Dip the brush in the medium green paint (it should be a few shades lighter than the dark green). Do not load the

brush with paint; rather, keep it slightly "dry." Lightly drag the brush over the dark green paint, making random swirls, circles, and jiggles as you move across the surface. Allow to dry.

3. Sand the bottom part of the chest with a fine sandpaper, then seal it with two coats of clear shellac, allowing the first coat to dry thoroughly before applying the second coat. (For this piece, there was no need for a colored base coat, since the original brown color made a good base color for the gold.)

4. Apply the leaf size and allow it to become tacky.

5. Apply the gold leaf, using full sheets. Leaf one side of the chest at a time, then the drawers, the legs, and the underside. Tamp the leaf into place with the camel hair brush after you lay the leaf.

6. Let the leaf dry overnight, then brush off the excess leaf. Lightly burnish the leaf by gently rubbing the leafed surfaces with a chamois.

7. Apply two coats of orange shellac, allowing the first coat to dry thoroughly before applying the second coat.

8. Finish and seal the top and bottom of the chest by applying two coats of gloss urethane. Allow to dry.

DESIGNER } **Happy Veirs**

Contemporary Japanese Box

Simplicity of form combines with a Japanese-inspired motif to create an elegant box. The gilded background and mother of pearl impart rich, quiet highlights to the overall effect.

If you do not want to use real gold leaf, you can try gold composition leaf, copper leaf, or variegated leaf in red or green.

MATERIALS

Box

Clear shellac

Resin (oil) varnish

Red acrylic paint

Gold leaf size

Gold leaf

Talcum powder

Washi paper (a decorative Japanese paper available in art supply shops)

Clear acrylic spray

Mother of pearl (available as flat sheets in art and craft supply shops)

Permanent black marker

White glue

Clear wood wax

TOOLS

Disposable foam brushes

#200, #400, #600 sandpaper

Brush for applying paint

Silk bob for applying size

1-inch (2.5 cm) sable brush

Scissors

Craft knife

Paper towels

Soft rags

INSTRUCTIONS

1. Apply two coats of clear shellac to the box's interior and exterior. Allow to dry.

2. Sand with #200 sandpaper.

3. Apply two coats of red paint. Allow to dry. Sand lightly with #600 sandpaper.

4. Apply one coat of the resin (oil) varnish. Allow to dry.

5. Using #400 and #600 sandpaper, sand until smooth.

6. Apply the leaf size with a silk bob.

7. Let the size dry until it is tacky to the touch (30 to 45 minutes).

8. Powder your hands with talcum powder. (Try to avoid touching the leaf with your bare hands.)

9. Apply the gold leaf.

10. Smooth the leaf with a soft sable brush or rouge paper that comes with the gold leaf.

11. Allow the gold leaf to dry thoroughly.

12. Seal the leaf with the varnish and allow to dry.

13. Beginning with the top of the box, cut a circular design out of the washi paper. Cut stripes from the center of the design to allow the mother of pearl to show through.

14. Spray the paper design with clear acrylic spray coat.

15. Using a sharp craft knife, cut the mother of pearl to fit the design. Then, using the black marker, color the back of the mother of pearl to highlight the beautiful colors.

16. Repeat Steps 13 through 14 for each side of the box.

17. Using white glue, glue the mother of pearl to the box first. Allow the glue to dry. Next, glue the cut-out paper design.

18. Use paper towels dampened with lukewarm water to remove any excess glue or glue drips. Let dry.

19. Apply 25 coats of varnish with a disposable foam brush, allowing the varnish to dry thoroughly between coats. Then sand with #400 or #600 sandpaper.

20. Apply five more coats of varnish. Sand again until smooth.

21. Wax and polish the box with a soft cloth.

22. Finish the inside of the box by cutting the washi paper to fit. Glue the paper to the inside of the box, then varnish.

NOTE: To protect the box's interior and hold the top on when closed, a lucite liner was made for the bottom of the box that extends $\frac{1}{4}$ inch (.5 cm) above the inside height measurement.

Hat

Sometimes all it takes is a new way of looking at something to brighten your total outlook. If you just can't seem to get around those big obstacles in life, have fun transforming what you can. This plain, black felt hat becomes a bright accessory with the addition of gold leaf, feathers, and bows.

DESIGNER } **Dyan Mai Peterson**

MATERIALS

Black felt hat (this one came
    from a resale shop)
Acrylic-based gesso or acrylic
    gloss medium
Acrylic artist's color
Leaf size
Composition gold leaf
Copper leaf
Silver leaf
Acrylic varnish
Feathers
Ribbon
White glue

TOOLS

Disposable foam brushes
Artist's brushes
Scissors
Small round-head sewing pins

INSTRUCTIONS

1. Prepare the hat by removing any decorations. (This hat had a net over the crown, which was removed and saved for replacement after gilding.)

2. Using a disposable foam brush and either white acrylic gesso or clear acrylic gloss medium, seal the porous fibers of the cloth on the crown and brim of the hat so they will accept the size. If you have white acrylic gesso, you can mix the white gesso with pigments to closely match the color of the hat. Or you can use the white gesso, allow it to dry, then apply a base coat of acrylic artist's color. Using the clear gloss medium will allow the color of the hat to show through.

3. Apply the leaf size to the gessoed areas of the hat with a disposable foam brush. When the size becomes tacky, apply the leaf, pressing it into place with the tissue paper that comes with the leaf. Three different colors of leaf were used for this project to create the effect. Allow to dry.

4. Using a soft brush, brush off the excess leaf.

5. Seal the leaf with the clear acrylic varnish.

6. Now you can decorate the hat as you please. You can do countless treatments using ribbon, flowers, feathers, pins, and white glue. For this hat, the net was replaced on the crown. A gold ribbon was measured to the circumference of the crown, cut, and glued at the center back with white glue. The feathers were inserted into the hat band and glued in place. A gold bow was made out of the same ribbon as the hat band. It was tied onto the hat band and secured in place with white glue and pins.

Wearables

DESIGNER } **Susan Kinney**

Polymer Clay Necklace and Earrings

The black and gold of this necklace and earrings make a dramatic statement. No one would ever guess how simple they are to make.

You can use this project as the basis for almost endless variations. By changing the color of the clay, the type of leaf, or the shape of the beads, you can create wardrobes of interesting jewelry to keep or give away.

MATERIALS

One package of black polymer clay
Five sheets of composition gold leaf
Thin leather cord
Quick-drying, strong glue
Earring backs

TOOLS

Darning needle or piercing tool

INSTRUCTIONS

1. Condition and warm the clay by kneading it with your hands until it is pliable.

2. For the necklace, create a set of graduated size beads by rolling the clay into small balls.

3. For the earrings, roll six small beads. Flatten two of these to accommodate the earring backs.

4. Roll all the beads in torn composition gold leaf. Do not cover the beads completely; let the black show through.

5. Pierce each bead with the darning needle or piercing tool.

6. Bake the beads according to the clay manufacturer's instructions.

7. For the necklace, string the beads onto the cord, making a simple knot on each side of each bead. Arrange the beads as you wish, leaving pleasing spaces between them.

8. For the earrings, string the small beads as for the necklace. Make sure the flattened beads are on the top.

9. Glue the earring backs to the flattened beads.

Gold Leaf and Decoupage Oriental Pin

When decoupage is combined with gilding, a simple shell becomes a lovely, iridescent pin in a few short steps.

DESIGNER } **Happy Veirs**

MATERIALS

Shell
Red acrylic paint
Leaf size
Composition gold leaf
Resin (oil) or water-based varnish
Print for decoupage
Clear acrylic spray coat
White glue
Jewelry pin
Epoxy glue

TOOLS

Paint brush
Scissors
Paper towels
#400 and #600 sandpaper

INSTRUCTIONS

1. Since the shell is smooth, directly apply the red acrylic paint. Allow to dry.

2. Apply the gold size. When tacky (30 to 45 minutes), apply the gold leaf or composition leaf. Allow to dry thoroughly.

3. Apply the resin (oil) varnish or the water-based varnish. Allow to dry.

4. Cut out the print of your choice. Seal it with a coat of clear acrylic spray. Decide where you will place it on the shell.

5. Glue the print to the shell using the white glue. Clean up any drips with a damp paper towel. Allow to dry.

6. When the glue is dry, begin applying the varnish. Apply five to seven coats, allowing each coat to dry thoroughly before applying the next coat.

NOTE: Do not mix varnishes. If you used an oil varnish in Step 3, you must use an oil varnish for this step. Likewise, if you used a water-based varnish in Step 3, you must use a water-based varnish for this step.

7. Sand lightly with the #400 or #600 sandpaper to smooth out the surface. If you want the pin to be very shiny, do not sand.

8. Glue the jewelry pin on the back with a strong epoxy glue.

Gilded Gourd Jewelry

Gourds to wear! While gourds are most often thought of as vessels, their hard and durable skins provide a perfect material for surface decoration.

MATERIALS

One small gourd

Water-based size

Composition gold leaf

Leather dye in black and British tan colors*

Clear satin finish spray lacquer

Small bronze bugle beads

Matte colored beads

Black lacing thread

Household cement

Hypo-allergenic earring backs for pierced or unpierced ears

* You can purchase leather dye from a leather supply company, craft store, or shoe repair shop.

TOOLS

Small hand saw

Three brushes:
one for applying size
one soft brush for removing excess leaf
1-inch (2.5 cm) water color brush for applying leather dye

Small craft drill, either hand or power, or small awl

INSTRUCTIONS

1. Clean the gourd as outlined on page 82.

2. Using the small saw, cut abstract shapes from the gourd: a larger rectangle for the necklace, smaller rectangles for the earrings. For the bracelets, cut rings from the neck of the gourd, making sure the circumference of each ring is sufficient to slip over the hand.

3. Apply the size randomly to the surfaces where you want to lay the leaf.

4. Once the size becomes tacky, apply the leaf. Brush off the excess leaf with the soft brush.

5. Using a brush, apply the black leather dye where you want it, painting it just up to the edges of the gold leaf. Next apply the tan leather dye in the remaining areas, covering some or all of the gold leaf. Allow to dry.

6. Brush a coat of the black leather dye on the backs of the necklace and earrings and on the inside surfaces of the bracelets. Allow to dry.

7. For the first sealer coat, apply a fine mist of clear, satin-finish spray lacquer. Allow to dry. Apply two to three more coats, allowing each coat to dry thoroughly before applying the next one. Be careful not to use too much lacquer in any one coat; it will run and create drips.

8. Using the small hand drill or awl, make two holes for attaching the beaded necklace straps.

9. Bead the black lacing threads and then attach them to the gilded necklace piece.

10. Glue the earring backs to the wrong side of the earrings.

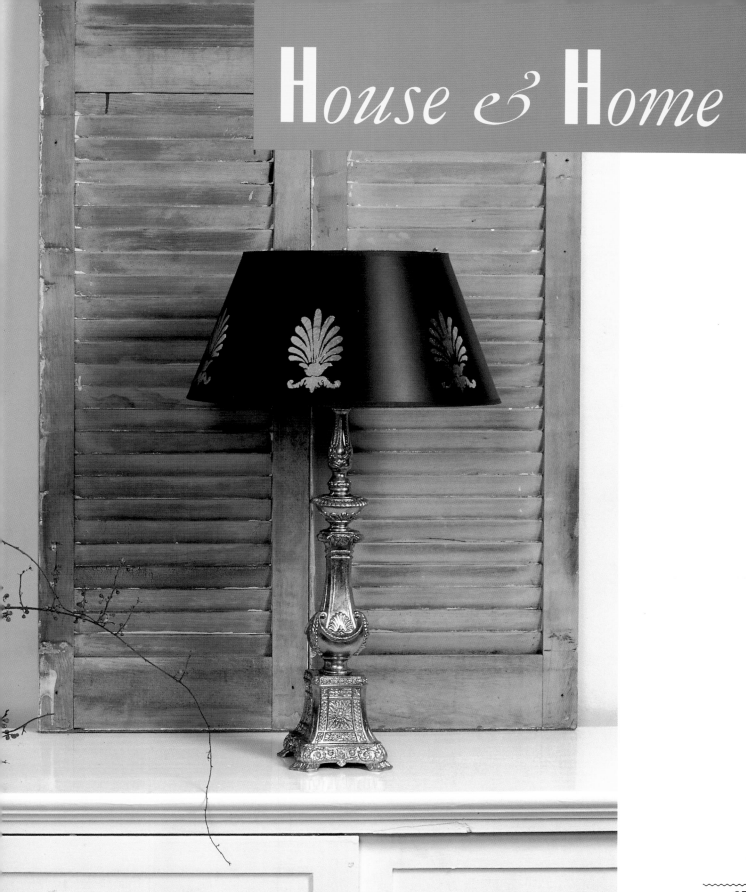

House & Home

DESIGNER } **Gay Grimsley**

Metal Lamps With Stenciled Shades

The original finish on these lamps had worn away, prompting the owner to send them to the flea market. Their classic style, however, did not escape the eye of the gilder. Variegated leaf on the bases and composition gold on the shades have given them a stunning new appearance.

MATERIALS

Metal lamp bases

Metal polish

Rust-inhibiting spray primer

Gold spray paint (or color of choice)

Water-based size

Two books of variegated composition gold leaf *

Heavy paper lamp shades, either recycled or new

Heavy drawing paper or ready-made stencil

Clear shellac

Leaf sealer (commercial preparation) or clear varnish (either oil or acrylic)

* Variegated leaf is readily available through leaf supply companies.

TOOLS

Wire brush

1-inch (2.5 cm) bristle brush for size and sealer

1-inch (2.5 cm) soft, natural-hair artist's brush

½-inch (1.5 cm) soft, natural-hair artist's brush

Craft knife

Cheesecloth

Low-tack masking tape (stencil tape)

Foam rubber cosmetic wedge

INSTRUCTIONS

1. Prepare the metal surface by using a wire brush and metal polish to remove any rust or corrosion.

2. Spray the lamps with rust-inhibiting metal primer. Allow to dry thoroughly.

3. Spray the lamps with the metallic gold paint or the color of your choice. This is the base coat that will show through the cracks in the leaf. Either black, dark red, or dark green base coats would provide handsome highlights. Allow to dry thoroughly.

4. Brush on the leaf size with a bristle brush. Make sure to cover the entire surface. Be careful not to leave any drips or puddles in the crevices. Allow the size to dry about one hour until clear and tacky.

5. Cut or tear the variegated leaf into workable-sized pieces. Tearing a whole leaf into two to three smaller pieces works well. Using a whole piece of leaf at one time can be very wasteful when working on a raised surface. Smaller pieces of leaf are much more manageable for leafing crevices.

6. Carefully lay the leaf onto the surface and gently tamp it down with a very soft, 1-inch (2.5 cm), natural-hair artist's brush (hard bristles will scratch the leaf). Use a smaller ½-inch (1.5 cm) brush if necessary. Brush off the excess leaf and save the skewings for later on.

7. Continue laying the leaf, slightly overlapping the pieces until the entire surface is covered.

8. If there are any places you missed, use the skewings to fill in the cracks. This is called "faulting."

9. If there are areas where the leaf hasn't adhered, of if there are larger cracks than desired, go back and spot apply the size over these areas. Allow to dry until tacky and apply more leaf.

10. Allow the piece to dry completely until all tacky areas are gone. Buff with cheesecloth to remove any stray pieces of leaf. (If there are any tacky areas left before buffing, the fibers of the cloth will adhere to the piece.)

11. Brush on two coats of leaf sealer or clear oil or acrylic varnish. Let the first coat dry completely before applying the second coat.

LAMP SHADES

1. Prepare the shade surface if needed by applying a base coat of acrylic paint in a desired color. Spray paint, when applied according to the manufacturer's directions, will provide a nice smooth surface.

2. Coat a heavy piece of drawing paper with clear shellac. Allow it to dry. Draw or trace a stencil design on the coated paper. Cut out the design with a craft knife. These lamp shades have a scallop shell design that mirrors a motif on the base. You can also use a ready-made stencil.

3. Tape the stencil to the shade, using a low-tack masking tape. Avoid using regular masking tape, which will damage the shade.

4. Use the cosmetic wedge to sponge the size into the cut openings of the stencil, making sure to fill all areas. Don't apply too heavily or the size will run under the stencil. Let dry until clear and tacky.

5. Apply leaf to the stenciled area and tap down with soft, natural-hair artist's brush. Brush off the excess leaf. Do not apply sealer to the gilded stencilled areas if the design is delicate. The sealer will get on the shade and ruin the effect.

DESIGNER } Terry Taylor

Gilded Eggs

Throughout history, the embellishment of the egg has always been a tribute to the perfection of its shape. Gilding lends rich highlights to these eggs, while added ornamentation creates interest.

MATERIALS

Wooden eggs and egg cups

Egg-shaped box of paper mache, plaster, or china

Assorted pieces of costume jewelry

Acrylic modeling paste

Acrylic primer (used as a base coat)

Acrylic gesso

Assorted colors of acrylic paints

Water-based size

Composition leaf (gold, silver, copper, variegated)

Wood glue

Antiquing glaze (commercial preparation available in craft supply shops)

Acrylic varnish

Spray sealer

Commercial preparation for creating a verdigris effect (optional)

TOOLS

Carving knife

Small chisels

Drill with small bit for wood

Sandpaper

Brushes

Small sea sponge (for sponge painting)

Wire cutter

Round-head map pins

Syringe (optional)

Soccer Shoes

Once baby shoes were bronzed as a sentimental memento. Why stop there? Immortalize a winning season, a completed marathon, or good sportsmanship with this very personal trophy.

DESIGNER } **Jane LaFerla**

MATERIALS

Shoes

Old newspapers

Acrylic gesso

Light cadmium red artist's acrylic
  paint

Water-based size

Gold composition leaf

Burnt sienna and raw umber ink

Gloss acrylic varnish

TOOLS

Two 2-inch (5 cm) disposable foam
  brushes

2-inch (5 cm) bristle brush

Soft, medium sized natural hair
  artist's brush

Pair of small pliers

INSTRUCTIONS

1. Remove the shoe laces. Stuff the toes of the shoes with newspaper so the shoes will retain their shape as you work.   Coat the shoe laces with a thin layer of gesso, let them dry and then apply another thin layer. Set the laces aside.

2. Leather or vinyl shoes are non-porous and will not need to be sealed. Fabric to be gilded on the inside or outside of athletic shoes will need to be sealed. This can be done by applying one layer of acrylic paint to the fabric, allowing it to dry, then applying a second layer.

3. Apply a base coat of acrylic paint. This may not always be necessary. These shoes were two-toned, and paint was applied to give them a uniform undercoat.

4. Using a disposable foam brush, apply the size to the bottom of the shoes. Wait for it to become tacky, then apply leaf. Any raised surfaces, such as cleats, will require several layers of leaf for complete coverage.

TIP: Use smaller pieces of leaf when working on raised surfaces. Cut the leaf between two layers of tissue paper before laying.

5. Brush the excess leaf from the bottom of the shoes, using the 2-inch (5 cm) brush.

6. Apply the size to any inside surface of the shoe that will be visible. Wait for it to become tacky and lay the leaf. Remember, if the inside is fabric, it will have to be sealed before it can accept the size. Brush off the excess leaf.

7. Apply the size to the outside of the shoe, wait for it to become tacky, and then, working from the bottom up, apply the leaf. Brush off the excess.

8. Apply the size to the tongue of the shoe, wait for it to become tacky, then apply the leaf, brushing off the excess.

9. Take the gesso-coated laces and lace the shoes as you would normally. The gesso makes the laces stiff. A pair of pliers will help pull the laces through.

10. Apply the size to the laces and bows, wait for it to become tacky, then apply the leaf. Several layers of leaf may be necessary to cover the raised surface of the laces. Brush off the excess leaf after each layer. Though the process is tedious, the finished effect makes the laces look as though they'd been cast in metal.

11. Let the leaf set for 24 hours.

12. To tone down the bright gold finish, apply a thin layer of burnt sienna ink with a soft brush. Let that dry, then apply a thin layer of raw umber ink.

13. When the ink is completely dry, use a disposable foam brush to apply a sealer coat of gloss acrylic varnish.

DESIGNER } **Sharon Tompkins**

Flower Pot

You can always use this gilded flower pot for planting, but think of some fun alternatives. Several small pots can be used as glittering candle holders to light up your patio on a summer's night. Or, you can fill a pot with seasonal goodies to give as an eat-now, plant-later gift.

MATERIALS

Terra cotta flower pot

Acrylic artist's paint

Water-based size

Composition gold leaf

Clear acrylic varnish (water-based)

Mahogany or walnut wood wiping stain
(do not use penetrating stain).

TOOLS

Disposable foam brushes

Artist's brushes

INSTRUCTIONS

Terra cotta has a smooth surface but it is porous. You can seal the pot and provide a colorful base coat at the same time by using acrylic artist's colors.

1. Paint the inside of the pot with deep blue acrylic paint. Paint the outside with red acrylic paint, which will serve as the bole. Allow to dry.

2. With a disposable foam brush, apply the size to the outside of the pot. Allow it to reach tack, then lay the leaf. If you like the "faults," keep them; if not, patch with your skewings. Allow the pot to dry overnight.

3. Brush off the excess leaf.

4. Apply two coats of clear acrylic varnish to the inside and outside of the pot, allowing the varnish to dry between coats.

Variation

Antique the pot with wood wiping stain by applying the stain and allowing it to fill the faults. Wipe off the excess. Allow the stain to dry, then apply two coats of clear acrylic varnish to seal.

Gilded Bowl

This nicely shaped bowl is as beautiful to hold as it is to admire. Once a plain, raku-fired vessel, it has gotten a second life with a textured surface underneath its new golden exterior.

DESIGNER **Susan Kinney**

MATERIALS

Small bowl
White glue
Tissue paper
Clear matte spray lacquer
Leaf size
Composition gold leaf
Black ink

TOOLS

Disposable foam brushes
Brush for ink
Soft, lint-free rag

INSTRUCTIONS

1. For the textured surface, brush the white glue on the outside of the bowl. Apply the tissue paper, wrinkling it as you go to create the desired amount and effect of the texture.

2. Spray the surface with clear matte lacquer to seal the paper so it will accept the size.

3. Apply the size to the bowl's exterior. Wait for it to become tacky, then apply the leaf. Allow to dry.

4. Spray the leaf with the clear matte lacquer.

5. When it's dry, brush with black ink, wiping off the excess with a rag until the desired shading is achieved.

6. Spray with the clear matte lacquer or brush on the gold leaf sealer.

NOTE: The textured surface is optional. You may prefer a smooth gilded surface for your project. Gilded bowls must be carefully hand-washed and are not dishwasher safe. They are not recommended for the preparation or serving of food.

DESIGNER } **Sally Bryenton**

Picture Gourd

By giving us gourds, Mother Nature has provided us with a perfect canvas. Use the gourd's surface for painting a picture that tells a story; add gilding, and you immediately illuminate your thoughts.

MATERIALS

Gourd

Water-based size

Composition gold leaf

Copper leaf

Composition silver leaf

Clear acrylic spray

TOOLS

Pencil

Medium-grit sandpaper

Steel wool

Wood-burning tool

Artist's brushes, one very soft

Orange stick or other small pointed stick

INSTRUCTIONS

1. Clean any debris from the surface of the gourd by gently rubbing with the sandpaper or steel wool.

2. Create or transfer a drawing on the surface of the gourd. Use a light touch so you will not make any indentations at this time.

3. When you are satisfied with your drawing, use a wood-burning tool to burn the lines of your drawing into the skin of the gourd.

4. With an artist's brush carefully apply the size to an area of the drawing. Avoid getting the size in the burned lines. Allow the size to reach tack and lay the leaf. Move on to another area, apply the size, and lay the leaf.

5. Use the three different varieties of leaf around the gourd. Each area of this gourd is double gilded. Allow each application of each leaf to dry completely.

6. Remove the excess leaf with a very soft artist's brush. If you see any faults, fill them in with your skewings.

7. Once the leaf is dry and the excess leaf removed, check the incised lines and remove any leaf with an orange stick or other small pointed stick.

8. Spray the entire surface of the gourd with clear acrylic spray to seal the copper and composition leaf.

The Gourd Kingdom

There are three types of gourds: the *cucurbita*, or ornamental; the *laginaria*, or hardshell; and the *luffa*, or vegetable sponge. The most common gourd used for decorating is the laginaria.

The blossoms of the plant are white and bloom at night. The gourds are green and need plenty of sun, space, and water as they grow. Because the gourds have a thick, hard shell and are 90 to 95% water, they may take six months to a year to dry. You can grow your own gourds or purchase them from a fruit stand or farmer's market.

Gilded Gourds

Artisans always have a way of turning functional objects into works of art. Since ancient times, gourds have been used as vessels for carrying water or storing food. Today, a new generation is discovering the beauty of working with gourds.

DESIGNER ⟩ Dyan Mai Peterson

MATERIALS

Cured and cleaned gourd

Wood filler

Water-based black spray enamel

Water-based size

Composition gold leaf

Leather dye in black, British tan, and mahogany colors *

Clear satin-finish spray lacquer

Black tassel

Gold bead

Skewings in copper, gold, and silver (whatever you have on hand)

* You can purchase leather dye from a leather supply company, craft store, or shoe repair shop.

TOOLS

Stiff scrubbing brush

Pencil

Small power or hand saw

Grapefruit spoon or scraping tool

Coarse and fine sandpaper

Three brushes:

  one for applying size

  a soft brush for removing excess leaf

  1-inch (2.5 cm) water color brush for applying leather dye

Paper plate

INSTRUCTIONS
Gourd With Lid

1. If the outside of the gourd is not clean, use warm water and a stiff brush to remove the dirt and mold. Be careful not to scratch the surface.

2. Decide which side of the gourd will be the front of the finished piece. With a pencil, draw a line around the top of the gourd; this will become your guide for cutting the lid. You can make a perfect circle with the help of a compass or draw an abstract, freehand line. You can also choose to leave the gourd whole.

3. On the lid line at the center back of the gourd, use a small saw to score a starting line for the first cut. Slowly cut back and forth. Now begin to cut all the way around. It will help to point your saw blade in the up and down position. If there are any gaps between the gourd and lid when you finish sawing, use wood filler to fill, let it dry, then sand with fine sandpaper.

4. Clean the inside of the gourd and lid, using a grapefruit spoon or scraping tool to remove the pulp and seeds.

5. Once the gourd is clean, use a coarse sandpaper on the inside wall, then use a fine sandpaper to further smooth the interior surface. Spray the inside with water-based, black enamel.

6. Starting at the outside front of the gourd, apply size randomly to the gourd where you want to lay the leaf. (This project has squares and triangles, but use your imagination!)

7. Once the size becomes tacky, apply the leaf. Brush off the excess leaf with a soft brush.

8. Using a brush, apply the black leather dye where you want it, painting it just up to the edges of the gold leaf shapes. Next, apply the tan leather dye in the remaining areas. You may also cover some or all of the gold leaf with the tan leather dye. Allow to dry.

9. For the first sealer coat, apply a fine mist of clear, satin-finish spray lacquer. Allow to dry. Apply two to three more coats, allowing each coat to dry thoroughly before applying the next one. Be careful not to use too much lacquer in any one coat, or it will run and create drips.

10. Add a tassel and bead to the stem. If your gourd does not have a stem, drill a hole in the center of the lid and thread the end of the tassel and bead through the hole. Make a large enough knot on the inside to prevent the end of the tassel from coming through the hole.

11. Sign and date your work. Happy gourding!

Whole Gourd

The whole gourd pictured is created in the same manner as the lidded gourd, except a mahogany-colored dye was used in place of the tan dye. It has the same effect, but imparts a burgundy color to the leaf.

Gourd Bowl

1. Following the instructions for the gourd with lid, cut and clean a small, round gourd into a bowl shape.

2. Coat the inside of the gourd with water-based, black spray enamel.

3. Randomly paint the gourd with the black leather dye. Leave spaces for the tan dye.

4. Paint the remaining areas with tan dye. Allow to dry.

5. With a brush, apply a ¾-inch (2 cm) stripe of size near the top of the bowl.

6. Place skewings on a paper plate. Roll the bowl in the skewings until the sized stripe is covered.

7. Seal the bowl with clear, satin-finish spray lacquer.

Pedestal

Transform an ordinary plaster pedestal into a functional work of art. The use of variegated copper composition leaf gives the piece a marbled effect for contemporary interest.

DESIGNER } **Gay Grimsley**

MATERIALS

Plaster pedestal

All-purpose primer/sealer

Gold leaf adhesive or water-based size

One book of variegated copper composition leaf

Leaf sealer or clear varnish

TOOLS

Fine sandpaper

Soft, natural-hair artist's brush

Cheesecloth

INSTRUCTIONS

1. Sand the pedestal with the fine sandpaper to get it as smooth as possible, paying special attention to any nicks or rough edges.

2. Prime the pedestal with the all-purpose primer/sealer to seal the porous plaster. Allow to dry.

3. Brush on the size, making sure to cover the entire surface. Stipple the size into the cracks and crevices of the pedestal. Allow the size to become tacky.

4. Lay whole pieces of leaf on the pedestal at a time, tamping them down with a soft artist's brush (use a natural-hair brush, since bristles will scratch the leaf). Continue overlapping the previous pieces until the surface is completely covered. Brush off the excess leaf and save the skewings for filling in any places that you might have missed.

5. Buff the surface with the cheesecloth.

6. Apply two coats of the leaf sealer, allowing each coat to dry thoroughly (approximately two hours) between coats.

NOTE: Another way to treat the pedestal is to apply a base coat of copper metallic spray paint. This pedestal was gilded on top of a white primer, which made all the cracks in the leaf much more noticeable, and the cracks needed more "faulting" to cover them.

DESIGNER Bernie Hauserman

Chow Empress Fire Screen

Free-standing representations of animals in costume, known as "dummy boards" or "mute companions," were popular as decorative accessories in the homes of 17th-century, Northern European aristocracy. This fire screen portrays a chow as empress dressed in an azurite-colored dragon robe with sungari pearls of the Qing Dynasty.

MATERIALS

Drawing paper
Tracing paper
½-inch (1.5 cm) cherry plywood
Flat black spray paint
Clear latex polyurethane varnish
Water-based size
Composition gold leaf
Black acrylic paint
Satin-finish leaf sealer
Acrylic paints
Clear gloss acrylic varnish
Walnut wood wiping stain

TOOLS

Band saw
Paint brushes for applying varnish
Fine grit sandpaper
2 pencils, one hard lead, one soft
Artist's brush for applying size
Sable brush
Bristle brush
Sponge
Paper towels

INSTRUCTIONS

Once you complete these preliminary steps, the process moves along rather swiftly. First, do the research that will lead you to the selection of the right dog and costume. Then, proceed to the creation of working drawings that will determine the shape of the board and provide you with a design for transfer to the prepared board. Copy your finished design on tracing paper.

1. Using the band saw, cut the outline of the design from ½-inch cherry plywood.

2. Coat the reverse side with flat-black spray paint. Seal the front with a coat of latex polyurethane varnish. Allow at least two hours drying time.

3. Carefully sand the surface to be decorated (the one that has been coated with polyurethane).

4. Transfer the design to the board. Do this by taking the tracing paper with your copied design and turning it over. Retrace your lines on this side with a soft lead pencil. Lay the side of the paper with this soft lead tracing against the board. Using a sharp, hard lead pencil, go over the lines of the design. When you're finished, remove the tracing paper. The lines of the design should now be visible on the board.

5. Working one section at a time, apply water-based size directly to the areas to be gilded. When you apply the size, it will be a milky white. Wait until it turns clear and becomes tacky before applying the leaf.

6. Apply the leaf with a fat sable brush. Static electricity should enable you to pick up one sheet at a time. If this doesn't work, pick up the leaf with the tissue that separates the leaves and apply.

7. Using a soft brush, gently brush the leaf and let it dry for one-half hour.

8. Using a bristle brush, brush away excess leaf.

9. Outline the leafed areas with black acrylic paint.

10. Apply a satin-finish sealer to the leafed areas and allow to dry overnight.

11. At this point, paint the entire figure in full color. Since the gold leaf is meant to simulate gold embroidery, antique and shade the gold leaf on the costume. When the painting is completed to your satisfaction, coat the piece with clear gloss acrylic varnish and allow to hard dry overnight.

12. With a sponge, coat the painted side of the screen with walnut-colored stain. Determine which areas of the design you want to be lighter or darker. Then, using paper towels, carefully wipe the stain away. Leave more stain where you want it to remain dark and wipe away stain where you want it to remain light.

NOTE: This design does not have a colored base coat under the gold leaf. The antiquing and coloring of the gold leaf is done when the rest of the figure is painted.

DESIGNER } **Kathleen Burke**

Candlesticks

There are dozens of different looks for these candlesticks. You can combine gold and silver leaf, variegated leaf and composition gold, silver leaf patinated with prussian blue, copper leaf patinated with greens, or gold with black. The instructions given here are only the beginning.

MATERIALS

6-inch (15 cm) unfinished wooden candlesticks

Clear shellac

Red acrylic gesso

Leaf size

Variegated composition gold leaf

Gloss urethane

Two-step crackle varnish

Burnt umber oil paint

Linseed oil

TOOLS

Fine sandpaper

Brushes for applying shellac and gesso

Camel hair brush

Chamois

Soft, lint-free rags

INSTRUCTIONS

Variegated Candlesticks

1. Sand the wood lightly to remove any roughness.

2. Apply one coat of clear shellac. Allow to dry.

3. Apply two coats of the red acrylic gesso, sanding lightly between coats.

4. Seal with one to two coats of clear shellac.

5. Apply one thin coat of gold size.

NOTE: It is better to size and leaf smaller areas of an object at a time rather than trying to do the whole thing at once. Start by applying size, then leaf to the top half of the candlesticks, then apply size and leaf to the bottom half.

6. When the size has achieved the proper tack, apply the leaf. (Don't be concerned with small cracks; they are part of the charm.) Tamp the leaf down gently with the soft camel hair brush and allow to dry overnight.

7. Brush off the excess leaf and lightly burnish by gently rubbing the gilded surface with a chamois.

8. Apply two coats of gloss urethane.

Antique Patina Finish

1. Follow Steps 1 through 7 for the variegated candlesticks.

2. Following the manufacturer's instructions, apply the two-step crackle varnish. Allow to dry.

3. To create the patina, place a small amount of burnt umber oil paint that has been thinned with linseed oil on a soft rag and rub into the surface cracks of the varnish. With a clean rag, buff off the excess, leaving the most paint in the cracks and recesses of the candlestick.

4. Allow to dry for several days.

5. Apply two to three coats of urethane to seal.

NOTE: Use only oil paints for the patina. Acrylic paints will not give the effect you seek and should never be used for this process.

DESIGNER } **Jane LaFerla**

Gilded Roast Chicken

In 14th-century Europe, food was often gilded before it was served to the well off, because the alchemists of the time claimed that gold was a remedy for most ills of the body. While a gilded chicken may not cure your bodily ills, it will certainly elevate your spirits—and amaze your guests.

MATERIALS

Small roasting chicken, approx. 3 lbs (1.4 kg)

Poultry seasoning

One book of 23 karat edible gold

TOOLS

Heavy thread

Pastry brush

NOTE: You must use only the purest gold when working with food. The 23 karat gold used in this project is designated as edible because it contains mostly gold with a very small amount of silver. *Never* use composition leaf on food; its contents are poisonous.

INSTRUCTIONS

1. Prepare the chicken by seasoning inside the cavity. (You do not want any herbs or spices on the finished surface.)

2. Using the thread, truss the wings close to the body by circling around the back and breast several times. Truss the legs together until they are also close to the body.

3. Roast the chicken in a 350°F (176°C) oven until it is done, basting several times to ensure an even, golden-brown color.

4. Remove the chicken from the roasting pan and place on a serving platter.

5. Take the pan drippings and place them in a bowl.

6. Using the pastry brush, apply the drippings to a small area of the chicken (approximately the size of one leaf of gold).

7. Using the tissue paper from the book of gold, transfer a whole leaf of gold and apply it to the chicken. Continue applying the drippings to small areas of the chicken and leafing until the chicken is completely gilded. On the wings and legs it may be necessary to work very small areas at a time, cutting the leaf into smaller pieces between two pieces of tissue paper.

8. A variation on this recipe would be to use individual Cornish hens and gild as above.

Dining

Gilded Chocolate

Chocolate may be the absolute king of all confections, crowned by divine right to rule our senses and lead our appetites to undying allegiance. What better match for this monarch of delights than to be wedded to gold, which symbolizes wealth, goodness, and light?

DESIGNER } New World Chocolates

MATERIALS

Chocolate
Chocolate molds
One egg white
23 karat edible gold
Thick smooth cardboard

TOOLS

Small artist's brush
Soft artist's brush
Wax paper
Spoon

NOTE: You must use only the purest gold when working with food. The 23 karat gold used in this project is designated as edible because it contains only gold and a very small amount of silver. *Never* use composition leaf on food; its contents are poisonous.

INSTRUCTIONS

1. Use or find a favorite recipe for molding chocolates. Make and mold chocolates.

2. If you are not gilding the chocolates immediately after they're ready, store them in a cool, dry place. Do not store them in the refrigerator; the humidity will cause them to "sweat."

3. Make your own transfer leaf for easier handling. Begin by tearing a small sheet of wax paper and setting it aside.

4. Take the book of leaf and cut the binding edge to free the tissue paper. Grasp the sheet of tissue paper that is underneath the first gold leaf. Gently slide the tissue paper and gold leaf onto a piece of thick, smooth cardboard. (You do not want to move the leaf and tissue onto a hard surface.)

5. Carefully place the wax paper on the leaf and tissue. Using the rounded side of a spoon, gently rub the wax paper that is directly over the leaf. The leaf will stick to the wax paper, making the leaf easy to cut if necessary (cut with the wax paper side up, leaf side down) and easier to handle.

6. Place the white of one egg in a bowl or cup.

7. Using a small artist's brush, apply the egg white to the chocolate in the areas you want gilded. (Apply as evenly as possible, avoiding any puddles or dabs.)

8. Wait only until the egg white loses its sheen, then immediately apply the leaf that is stuck to the wax paper.

9. Carefully press the wax paper backing. The leaf should adhere to the egg white and separate from the wax paper. Using the soft artist's brush, tamp the gold into place, then gently brush away the excess leaf.

10. Allowing faults to remain is desirable when working with chocolate. The dark brown color of the chocolate is a beautiful contrast to the gold.

DESIGNER ⸭ Terry Taylor

Plates

Looking for a dramatic presentation for a dinner party or holiday? Imagine the shimmering glow of candlelight reflected off the gold, silver, and copper highlights of these plates.

MATERIALS

Glass plates
Acrylic paint
Water-based size
Composition leaf (gold, silver, copper)
Matte or gloss acrylic spray

TOOLS

Masking tape
Sea sponge
Small brushes

NOTE: These plates are designed to be used as chargers (decorative plates underneath smaller plates or bowls). Consequently, they may not need to be washed, only wiped clean.

INSTRUCTIONS
Large Plate

1. Using masking tape, mask the areas on the back of the plate where you don't want the paint to go. For this plate, mask off points on each segment of the rim.

2. Dampen a sea sponge. Dip it in a small amount of paint in a desired color. Lightly dab the sponge on the back of the plate to achieve a mottled effect. Allow to dry.

3. Remove the tape. Apply the size evenly to the back of the plate. Allow it to become tacky and then apply the leaf.

4. Gently rub the leaf smooth, using the tissue paper from the book of leaf or a soft brush. Use the skewings or small pieces of leaf to fill in any faults.

5. Lay the plate face down. Seal the leaf with several coats of acrylic spray, allowing the spray to dry between coats.

6. Hand wash the plates after use. Do not wash in dishwasher.

Small Plate

1. Use a small brush to apply the size in stripes to the back of the plate rim. When tacky, apply small amounts of gold leaf and wipe away the excess.

2. Repeat Step 1, using silver composition leaf

3. Apply sizing to entire plate back. When tacky, apply the copper leaf.

4. Seal the leaf with several coats of acrylic spray, allowing the spray to dry between coats.

5. Hand wash the plates after use. Do not wash in the dishwasher.

Basket

This basket was slated for the back of the closet. Now the rich, warm tones of copper leaf, combined with the interesting patterns of variegated leaf, have given it a new life.

DESIGNER } **Jane LaFerla**

MATERIALS

Basket
Clear shellac
Water-based size
Copper leaf
Green variegated leaf
Acrylic varnish

TOOLS

Two 2-inch (5 cm) disposable foam brushes
Two 2-inch (5 cm) bristle brushes

INSTRUCTIONS

1. If the basket is unpainted, seal it with clear shellac or paint it with acrylic paints. The paints will act as a sealer coat as well as the bole. This basket was already sealed with an antiqued, whitewashed finish. The red-beige undertone of the basket was the inspiration to use copper leaf.

2. Using one of the disposable brushes, apply water-based size to the inside of the basket and allow it to reach tack. The size should coat only the exterior surface of the ribs or stakes, allowing the leaf to highlight the weaving. Do not try to cover all the ins and outs.

3. Pick up the leaf with the tissue paper that separates the leaves and begin laying the leaf on the inside bottom of the basket. Gently press the leaf in place with tissue paper. Work up the sides. When the inside is completely leafed, use the bristle brush to remove the excess leaf.

4. Clear your work area of skewings, then apply size to the outside of the basket. When the size is tacky, begin applying leaf from the bottom of the basket up the sides. If you desire, you can leaf the outside bottom of the basket, but it is not necessary.

5. Once the outside is completed, use the brush to remove the excess leaf. Small skewings will get caught in the basket weave, and it may be necessary to brush the inside and outside several times to remove these. Clear area of skewings.

6. Apply size on random areas of the basket over the copper leaf.

7. When the size becomes tacky, lay smaller pieces of variegated leaf on the randomly sized areas. This gives the basket subtle highlights that complement the copper.

8. Brush off the excess variegated leaf.

9. Apply the size to the handle and wait for it to become tacky.

10. Cut the copper leaf between two sheets of tissue paper to make smaller, more manageable pieces for leafing the handle. Apply the leaf to the handle, pressing the leaf gently into place with the tissue paper. Allow the leaf to set for 24 hours.

11. Use a disposable foam brush to apply the gloss varnish. Begin with the inside of the basket and work to the outside.

Antiqued Silver Footstool

Prop up your feet and relax in style. The antiqued silver leaf on this footstool imparts a comfortable, lived-in look, perfect for the room where you're most at home.

MATERIALS

Footstool found at junk/antique shop

Water-based size

Silver composition leaf

Red mahogany and ebony waxed-wood finish (available in paint and hardware stores)

Fabric of choice

TOOLS

1-inch (2.5 cm) brush

Soft bristle brush for applying leaf

Clean rags

INSTRUCTIONS

1. Clean the wood surface. Apply the size with the 1-inch (2.5 cm) brush. Wait 30 minutes until it is tacky and ready to accept the leaf.

2. Pick up the leaf, using the tissue found between the leaves in the book. Gently lay the leaf on the sized surface.

3. Using a very soft bristle brush, gently press the leaf onto the surface. Allow the cracks to show through as desired.

4. To "dull" and "warm" the bright silver color, apply a colored, waxed-wood finish. For this piece, an ebony color is used to darken it, while a red mahogany color gives a warmer tone. Using clean rags, apply the finish unevenly for an antiqued effect.

5. If it is an upholstered piece, recover with a fabric of your choice.

NOTE: This piece wasn't painted before gilding so the dark, original finish would show through the cracks of the leaf. However, it could have been painted a dark or intense color for a different effect.

DESIGNER } **Maggie Rotman**

Plant Stand

The golden frogs resting on the lily pads of this plant stand are sure to catch the light from any sunny window. Without a plant, the stand can serve as a whimsical accent table in any room.

MATERIALS

Unpainted plant stand

Flat latex paint

Chrome green and cadmium red light artist's acrylics

Heavy paper or cardboard

Acrylic gesso

Red artist's oil paint

Leaf size

Composition gold leaf

Clear matte polyurethane varnish

TOOLS

#400 sandpaper

Paint brush for applying paint

Pencil

Scissors

Three artist's brushes (one a fine size #2)

Soft lint-free cloth

INSTRUCTIONS

1. Prepare the stand by sanding with sandpaper.

2. Paint the stand, using a flat latex paint. (A cool, putty grey was selected for this project.)

3. Because water-based paint will raise the grain, sand after the paint dries, using a fine (#400) sandpaper. After sanding you may need to apply another coat of latex paint. If you do, sand again after the second coat dries.

4. Using artist's acrylics in the colors chrome green and cadmium red light, paint water lilies on the top and bottom shelf of the stand.

5. Design a frog motif that you would like to use on your stand. This project uses a simple outline of a frog.

6. Create a template of your design by taking heavy paper or cardboard and drawing the outline of your motif. Using scissors, cut it out. Decide where you want your frogs to appear on the lily pads. Place the template at one of these spots and trace around the outside of the template with a pencil. Continue moving and tracing the template until you have your desired number of frogs.

7. Using the #2 artist's brush, apply the gesso inside the outline of the frogs until the surface is slightly raised. This will take two or three applications. Allow the gesso to dry between each application. When you've applied all the layers, allow the gesso to dry overnight.

8. Sand the gessoed frogs with a fine-grit sandpaper (#400) until they are smooth.

9. Apply a coat of red artist's oil paint to the frogs and allow to dry thoroughly.

10. Apply the leaf size. Allow it to reach tack, then gently press a sheet of patent (transfer) composition gold leaf on the frogs. Do not rub at this point. Allow the leaf to dry several hours, then gently rub off any loose leaf with the soft cloth. Pay particular attention to the outline of the frogs, removing any gold leaf gently from their edges until clean.

11. You can use the leaf size as a varnish over the composition leaf to protect it from scratches and tarnishing. Allow to dry.

12. If desired, a coat of clear matte polyurethane varnish may be applied over the whole stand as a protective finish.

Copper Leaf and Stencilled Pine Table

Even a simple small table can become a standout when it's been decorated with stencils and leaf. Here, red is a natural complement to the copper leaf, while spatter-painting lends interest to the surface design.

DESIGNER **Kathleen Burke**

MATERIALS

Unfinished pine table

Clear shellac

Red acrylic gesso

Acrylic paint in black and metallic gold colors

Satin-finish urethane varnish

Leaf size

Copper leaf

Stencil

TOOLS

Fine sandpaper

Paint brushes for applying shellac and varnish

Newsprint *

Painter's tape *

Old toothbrush

Camel hair brush

Chamois

Fine steel wool

* Painter's tape is a low-tack tape and will not harm the surface. Use newsprint rather than old newspapers so there will be no chance of ink transfer.

1. Using fine sandpaper, lightly sand the table.

2. Seal the table with one coat of the clear shellac. Allow to dry.

3. Apply two coats of the red acrylic gesso to the entire table, sanding lightly between coats.

4. Seal the top of the table and the drawer front only with one coat of clear shellac. Allow to dry.

5. Using newsprint and tape, mask off the top and the drawer front.

6. Dip the bristles of the toothbrush in the black acrylic paint. Hold the toothbrush, bristle side up, close to the table. Run your thumb over the bristles of the brush. Allow the black acrylic paint to dry. Repeat this process using the metallic gold paint.

7. Using newsprint and tape, mask off the areas of the table that you want to remain red.

8. Apply two coats of the black acrylic paint to the legs for the base coat.

9. Following the technique described in Step 6, spatter the legs with red gesso. Allow to dry. Then spatter again, using the metallic gold paint. Allow to dry thoroughly.

10. Seal all the painted areas with two coats of the satin-finish urethane.

11. Remove the newsprint and masking tape from the top and drawer front. Apply one coat of gold size. When it achieves tack, lay down the copper leaf in full sheets. Tamp the leaf down with a soft, camel hair brush. Let the leaf dry overnight.

12. Brush off the excess leaf and lightly burnish by gently rubbing with the chamois.

13. LIGHTLY rub the steel wool over the top and drawer front in the direction of the grain to reveal some of the red base coat.

14. Seal the leaf with one coat of clear shellac and allow to dry.

15. Stencil the table using a pre-cut stencil or one of your own design. To paint the stencil, follow the spatter technique used on the rest of the table, using two colors of your choice selected from the black paint, metallic gold paint, or red gesso.

16. When the paint is dry, seal the top and drawer front with two to three coats of satin-finish urethane.

DESIGNER } **Sharon Tompkins**

Garden Room

With Copper Leaf-Accented Floor and Bronze Powdered Highlights

Gild your world! Don't just limit the application of leaf to small objects. For an interesting addition to any painted interior, incorporate leaf into your color scheme.

You can apply leaf to walls, moldings, door frames, and even floors. This project uses bronze powders for hard-to-leaf places and as a way to add extra sparkle to the walls.

This room has a large diamond painted on the floor. The points of the diamond are accented with copper leaf. The upper trim of the baseboard is painted with copper bronze powder and the sponged walls are highlighted with copper bronze powder that has been mixed into an acrylic gloss medium.

MATERIALS

Latex paints

Acrylic gloss medium

Copper bronze powder
(See Note at end of instructions.)

Water-based size

Metallic gold lining pen

Copper leaf

Acrylic varnish

TOOLS

Paint brushes

Paint rollers

Paint tray

Natural sea sponge

Sable artist's brushes

Straightedge

Low-tack masking tape

Painter's mask or respirator

INSTRUCTIONS

1. Design your room. As you do this, think of ways to unify the scheme by carrying the leaf color throughout the room.

2. Prepare all the room's surfaces for painting.

3. If necessary, paint the ceiling first. Then, paint the walls using a sponge technique. Begin by choosing three colors that coordinate with each other within your color scheme. Using brushes and a roller, apply the lightest color to the walls. This will be your base coat and will be the color you will see the least on the finished wall. Allow it to dry overnight. Using a natural sea sponge, apply the medium color over the base coat. Dab the paint on; don't drag the sponge across the surface. Allow this coat to dry. Apply the third color as you did the second coat. Allow to dry. Mix the copper bronze powder slowly into a gloss medium until you achieve the density you desire. You do not want to make opaque copper paint, rather, you want the mixture to be translucent, a "wash" of shimmering copper. Using a sea sponge, dab the copper mixture randomly on the wall as a highlight.

4. Paint the baseboards with latex paint in the color of your choice. Allow to dry.

5. Apply water-based size to the details of the baseboard that you will be gilding. Allow the size to reach tack.

6. With a sable artist's brush, apply the dry bronze powder directly to the sized baseboard (this is known as flash gilding). Allow to dry. You should use a painter's mask or respirator when working with bronze powders for extended lengths of time in confined areas.

7. Seal the baseboards with water-based varnish.

8. Lay out the floor design, using a straightedge for drawing the lines. Use a low-tack masking tape before and during painting to mask areas of your design as necessary.

9. Paint the floor with latex paint in the colors of your choice. Paint one area of the design at a time, allowing each area to dry thoroughly before moving to the next. For this project a metallic gold lining pen was used to highlight the design.

10. Apply the water-based size to the areas of the design to be gilded. Allow the size to reach tack.

11. Lay the leaf. Allow to dry overnight. Brush off the excess leaf.

12. Remove any skewings before sealing the floor.

13. Seal the floor with at least three coats of acrylic varnish, allowing each coat to dry thoroughly before applying the next coat. Oil-based paint and varnish are more durable and are recommended for floor applications. However, acrylic-based varnish was necessary for this project because the metallic gold lining pen contained an oil-based ink, and the oil-based varnish would act as a solvent to this ink, smearing the line.

NOTE: Bronze powders must be used with caution. They are fine powdered metal. As you breathe, they are taken into your system. You should wear a painter's mask when working with them. If you are using these powders for an extended period of time or are working in a confined space, you should use a painter's respirator.

Safer alternatives to bronze powders are mica powders. They are non-toxic, environmentally safe, and follow the same applications as bronze powders.

Parson's Table

This project is unique since its "leaf" is really paper-backed gold-foil gift wrap. Who would guess that underneath this surface lurks a white, molded-plastic table? Now, as a new casual piece, the table fits perfectly on a covered porch or deck.

DESIGNER } **Fred Gaylor**

MATERIALS

Plastic Parson's table

Red oxide spray metal primer

White glue (the thicker preparations found in craft stores work best)

Print or image of choice

Paper-backed gold-foil gift wrap

Burnt umber water-based antiquing medium (found in craft supply shops)

Spray acrylic sealer

Matte decoupage medium (found in craft supply shops)

TOOLS

Fine grit sandpaper

Soft, lint-free rag

Craft knife

INSTRUCTIONS

1. Lightly sand the table.

2. Spray the table with the red-oxide metal primer. Several coats of primer may be required to totally cover the table.

3. Glue the print or image of your choice to the center of the table top with craft glue.

4. Tear the paper-backed gold foil into square shapes. Don't be concerned that the shapes be uniform; you want a rough-edged look.

5. Beginning with the legs, glue the torn paper squares to the table with the thick craft glue. Leave thin spaces between the foil squares to allow the red base to show through, creating a mosaic effect.

6. As you work, use a damp rag to smooth the foil and remove any excess glue. Rinse the rag frequently in water as you burnish the surface.

7. Apply the squares in the same manner to the table top. Begin by laying the squares flush to the edges of the center design. Work down over the aprons of the table.

8. Use a craft knife to trim any excess off the bottoms of the table's aprons.

9. Use the damp rag to smooth the paper and remove the excess glue.

10. Allow the table to dry thoroughly.

11. Apply a thin mixture of water-based antiquing medium in a burnt umber color to the gold areas of the table.

12. Immediately wipe the medium off with a damp rag. This will tint the torn edges of the paper, which are white, and tone down the gold color. Allow to dry thoroughly.

13. When dry, apply several coats of matte decoupage medium to the table, sanding between coats.

14. Apply another coat of antiquing medium for an aged look. Allow it to dry.

15. Spray the table with two coats of acrylic sealer, allowing the sealer to dry thoroughly before applying the next coat. This will give the table a durable, waterproof surface.

Marble-Top End Table

These tables were flea-market finds that had already been stripped and were waiting for a wonderful finish. You can see the transformation in the "before" and "after" pictures.

DESIGNER } **Kathleen Burke**

MATERIALS

Clear shellac

Off-white acrylic paint

Red acrylic gesso

Acrylic paints in various colors to simulate marble

Gloss urethane

Satin-finish urethane

Leaf size

Composition gold leaf

Orange shellac

Oil paint in burnt umber color

TOOLS

Fine sandpaper

Brushes for applying paint

Painter's tape

Newsprint

Sponges

Brush for applying size

Camel hair artist's brush

Chamois

INSTRUCTIONS

1. If necessary, remove any old finish. Sand until smooth. The legs were purposefully left a bit rough so the gold wouldn't look too perfect.

2. Seal the wood with two coats of clear shellac.

3. Apply a base coat of off-white acrylic to the top and shelf.

4. Apply two coats of red acrylic gesso to the legs as a base coat. When dry, mask off the legs using newsprint and tape to protect the gesso base coat while you paint the top and shelf.

5. To achieve the marble effect, use a variety of sponges, brushes, and crumpled newsprint to layer on five different colors of acrylic paint.

6. When dry, seal the top and shelf with three to five coats of gloss urethane. This will give the surface depth. If you want less shine, the last two coats should be satin-finish urethane.

7. When dry, mask off the top and shelf with newsprint and tape to protect them as you gild the legs. Then seal the legs with two coats of clear shellac. Allow to dry thoroughly.

8. Apply gold size to the first leg you will be gilding. (It is best to gild one leg at a time.)

9. When the size is tacky to the touch, apply the gold leaf and tamp it into the recesses with the camel hair brush.

10. Gild the other leg. Allow the leaf to dry overnight.

11. Brush off the excess leaf. Burnish the leaf by gently rubbing it with a chamois.

12. If desired, you can patina the leaf to make it less bright. You can do this by applying a thin coat of orange shellac and letting it dry. Or, if you prefer, you can mix a glaze of burnt umber oil paint and orange shellac, apply a thin coat, and brush it so there is a hint of color on the surface and more color in the recesses.

13. When dry, seal the legs with two coats of satin-finish urethane.

Antiqued Gilded Chair

Just a hint of gold is all it takes to make this chair the focus of any room. The classic lines are toned with an antiqued finish and accented with antiqued composition leaf.

DESIGNER } **Sharon Tompkins**

MATERIALS

Chair

Wood filler

Clear shellac

Alkyd (oil) paint and oil glaze or commercial antique finish (oil base)

12-hour oil size

Composition gold leaf

Walnut or mahogany wood wiping stain

Clear satin-finish oil varnish

Mineral spirits

TOOLS

Medium and fine sandpaper

Tack cloth

Brushes for applying shellac and varnish

Brush for applying the size

Soft, lint-free rags

INSTRUCTIONS

1. Remove the old finish from the chair if necessary. (This always produces better final results.)

2. Fill in any holes and small nicks with the wood filler. Sand the chair first with medium grit sandpaper, then with fine sandpaper. Use a tack cloth to clean the surface. Seal the wood with a coat of clear shellac.

3. Create an antique finish for the chair, using your choice of commercial preparations (they are found in paint and hardware stores). Allow to dry.

4. Apply the size to the details you want gilded. Allow it to become tacky, then lay the leaf. Allow to dry.

5. Brush off the excess leaf.

6. Using a brush, apply the wiping stain in either mahogany or walnut finish to the details that have been gilded.

7. With a soft, lint-free rag, wipe off the amount of stain necessary for the desired effect. The more stain you remove, the lighter the antiqued tones. Allow to dry.

8. Apply two coats of satin-finish oil varnish, allowing it to dry thoroughly between coats.

9. Clean up using mineral spirits.

NOTE: You may use water-based paints and varnish. However, do not use oil-based paint products with water-based paint products. Be consistent in your choice, using either one or the other on any given project.

Contributing Designers

GRACE BAGGOT has shared a successful restoration business with her husband in New York City for the past 20 years. In addition, she has opened Baggot Leaf Company, which specializes in gilding supplies. Her personal interest is in Celtic art and history.

BESS BAIRD delights in gilding anything in front of her, especially the unusual. She immerses herself in visual delights by painting wall murals, sculpting with wood, and working with polymer clay.

LESLIE BOAN and **LUCINDA CARLSTROM** collaborate on mixed-media constructions and quilts. They are producing a series of pieces for spiritual and liturgical applications.

SALLY BREYENTON is currently designing and producing contemporary enamel jewelry. She is an artist who enjoys experimenting with different mediums and is a talented decorative painter.

BARBARA BROZIK has created art in many different forms, such as silkscreen prints, handmade cast paper constructions, and water-colored collages. Now she "creates fresh statements drawn from the past" in her painted furniture.

KATHLEEN BURKE started her own mural company while in college. Her painstaking work as a restorer of antique paintings is balanced by her love of creating faux finishes and decorative surfaces.

FRED GAYLOR is a versatile artist–designer who develops products for decorative giftware distributors. He enjoys staying busy by applying his extensive skills to any interesting project.

LAURIE GODDARD transforms the copper, silver, and composition leaf she applies to wood surfaces into patinated designs through processes she describes as "reverse alchemy." This decorative painter and designer from Connecticut has been experimenting with leaf for eight years.

GAY GRIMSLEY has her own business selling one-of-a-kind painted and gilded furniture and accessories. She specializes in faux finishes and stenciling.

JANET HANCHEY, who lives and works in New York City, specializes in the restoration of gilded surfaces. She particularly likes unravelling the mysteries of original recipes and applications. Her work can be seen at the New Amsterdam Theater, the Metropolitan Museum of Art, and the New York Public Library.

BERNIE HAUSERMAN was once a vice-president of visual merchandising. Now, he gives his limitless creativity full rein as creator of fanciful, hand-painted interior accessories.

SUSAN KINNEY puts her formal art background to use in a variety of fields. She is an interior designer who also creates polymer clay jewelry, raku pottery, and handmade paper.

SUSAN LIGHTCAP is a paper and book artist whose books and sculptural works are shown extensively in galleries across the country. Her work with books allows her to share her interests as a lifelong reader and journal keeper with many people.

NEW WORLD CHOCOLATES was begun by Chef Mark Rosenstein, owner of the nationally acclaimed Market Place Restaurant in Asheville, North Carolina. New World Chocolates provides a contemporary approach to the traditional craft of the chocolatier.

DYAN MAI PETERSON is a gourd artist whose fertile mind produces ideas as fast as a gourd vine produces blossoms in June. In addition to her gourd business, she teaches gourd making, is a basket maker, and runs her own mail-order bird-toy business.

JUNCO SATO POLLACK, fiber artist, teaches at Georgia State University in Atlanta. Her most recent work takes its inspiration from Zen calligraphy, landscape painting, and American Abstract Expressionism.

MAGGIE ROTMAN is a painter, currently working in watercolor. She is also an accomplished seamstress who enjoys designing and making clothes, slipcovers, and window treatments.

MARGERY SHERRILL is a decorative painter and restorer. Her work includes trompe l'oeil and gilding. She works in collaboration with her husband, Michael, gilding the teapots he produces.

MICHAEL SHERRILL is a self-taught ceramic artist whose work is in both public and private collections, including the White House Collection of American Craft.

RANDY SHULL has been a furniture artist "forever." His home and studio are in Asheville, North Carolina. His work can be seen at the American Craft Museum in New York City, the Brooklyn Museum, and the High Museum of Art in Atlanta.

LAURA SIMS has her own business as a marbler of paper and fabric. In her spare time, she shares her enthusiasm and love of the craft by teaching marbling workshops and classes to all ages.

BRENT SKIDMORE is a furniture maker and woodworker. He has taught at Penland School of Crafts and has been a visiting artist lecturer at schools throughout the southeastern United States.

SHARON NARADO SLOAN has been involved in arts and crafts for 20 years, first as a fiber artist and now as a studio potter. Her functional and decorative works incorporate both hand-built and wheel-thrown techniques.

JILL STOWE has a background in portrait painting and design. She is a self-taught gilder who does decorative painting and enjoys experimenting with a variety of furniture finishes.

TERRY TAYLOR claims he will gild anything as long as it doesn't move. His many talents and interests inspire him to work in a wide variety of mediums.

SHARON TOMPKINS has literally worked from floor to ceiling and all points in between in her work as a decorative painter. She creates large interior environments as well as smaller decorative pieces with equal ease.

HAPPY VEIRS has been a decoupeur for 25 years. She is affiliated with the National Guild of Decoupeurs and has achieved the status of Master Craftsman with the guild.

Acknowledgements

Special thanks to the Southern Highland Handicraft Guild; Village Antiques of Asheville, North Carolina; Gallery of the Mountains; and Grace Baggot of Baggot Leaf Company, New York, New York.

Index